Mastering Listening Skills

2

JN432929

Mastering Listening Skills Book 2

Publisher Chung Kyudo
Editors Kim Jinsuk, Cho Sangik
Author Michael A. Putlack
Designers Yoon Jiyoung, Park Sunyoung

First published in April 2014
By Darakwon, Inc.
Darakwon Bldg., 211, Munbal-ro, Paju-si, Gyeonggi-do 10881
Republic of Korea
Tel: 82-2-736-2031 (Ext. 250)
Fax: 82-2-732-2037

Copyright © 2014 Darakwon, Inc.

All rights reserved. No part of this publication may be reproduced, stored in a retrieval system, or transmitted in any form or by any means, electronic, mechanical, photocopying or otherwise, without the prior consent of the copyright owner. Refund after purchase is possible only according to the company regulations. Contact the above telephone number for any inquiries. Consumer damages caused by loss, damage, etc. can be compensated according to the consumer dispute resolution standards announced by the Korea Fair Trade Commission. An incorrectly collated book will be exchanged.

ISBN 978-89-277-0726-4 58740
978-89-277-0721-9 58740 (set)

www.darakwon.co.kr

Components Main Book / Workbook
14 13 12 11 10 9 8 25 26 27 28 29

Mastering Listening Skills

2

DARAKWON

Table of Contents

Introduction

Mastering Listening Skills Book 2 is the fourth book in a four-book series. This book is intended for intermediate learners of the English language. By using this book, learners will be able to improve their listening skills as well as their knowledge of English.

Mastering Listening Skills Book 2 contains twenty units. The twenty units are divided into five topics, each of which contains four units. The five topics in *Mastering Listening Skills Book 2* are Amazing Animals, Famous Journeys, American Folklore, Historical Mysteries, and Music. These are all topics that young learners find interesting and enjoy learning about. So learners will have fun listening to the material in this book while improving their English at the same time.

Every unit contains one main talk, a shorter talk, and questions about these talks. Each unit also contains a listening skill and exercises on it. The listening skills will help learners improve various aspects of their listening abilities.

Mastering Listening Skills Book 2 has several objectives. First, it will help learners improve their English abilities, particularly their listening skills. Next, it will teach them valuable knowledge about a wide range of academic topics. The talks themselves will also entertain learners as they listen to them. Finally, *Mastering Listening Skills Book 2* will help learners prepare for various standardized tests that they may take in the future. For instance, many questions about the talks are similar to those that appear on the iBT TOEFL® Junior and iBT TOEFL® exams. So, by using this book, learners should be able to get higher scores on the tests they take in the future.

About This Book

There are a total of twenty units. Each unit contains one main talk about a specific topic. There are vocabulary and listening comprehension questions about the main talk. There is also a shorter talk with listening comprehension questions. There are a total of ten listening skills that are taught in the various chapters. Finally, there is a comprehensive vocabulary section as well as a workbook that will help learners increase their understanding of the talks and improve their English abilities.

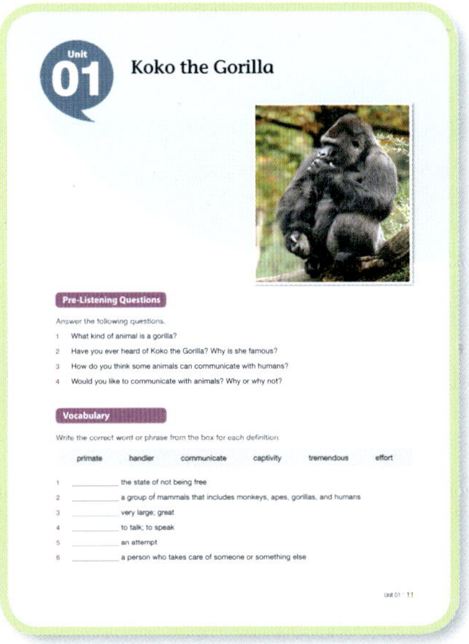

Unit 01 Koko the Gorilla

Pre-Listening Questions

Answer the following questions.

1 What kind of animal is a gorilla?
2 Have you ever heard of Koko the Gorilla? Why is she famous?
3 How do you think some animals can communicate with humans?
4 Would you like to communicate with animals? Why or why not?

Vocabulary

Write the correct word or phrase from the box for each definition.

primate handler communicate captivity tremendous effort

1 ________ the state of not being free
2 ________ a group of mammals that includes monkeys, apes, gorillas, and humans
3 ________ very large; great
4 ________ to talk; to speak
5 ________ an attempt
6 ________ a person who takes care of someone or something else

Unit 01 11

Pre-Listening Questions

There are four questions that focus on the picture or pictures at the top of the page. These questions will help prepare learners for the topic of the unit.

Vocabulary

This section contains six vocabulary words from the main talk. Learners should match the words with the definitions.

Talk

This is the main talk of the unit. Each talk is around 250-280 words long and focuses on the topic of the unit.

Organizer

This is a graphic organizer of the talk. There are six blanks for learners to fill in by using words in the talk.

Koko the Gorilla

Listen to the talk. Fill in the blanks as you listen.

Humans have long wanted to ________. They've been able to do this ________. For instance, ________ such as "Sit," "Come," and "Roll over." ________ can understand a small number of instructions. But animals ________ in any languages that people can understand.

Some scientists believed ________ such as gorillas and chimpanzees ________ though. They did this ________. It's also called ASL. ________ was Koko. The effort to teach Koko to talk with humans has been ________.

Koko was born ________ in 1971. She has spent ________. Koko is a western lowland gorilla. In 1976, the Gorilla Foundation was established. ________ two gorillas to communicate with humans by using ASL. Two gorillas were involved in the project: ________. Both learned ASL, but ________ than Michael.

In fact, Koko has learned more language than ________. She is ________ although she is rather old for a gorilla. She knows more than 1,000 signs, and she can understand more than ________. Her handlers believe her IQ is ________. 100 is average for humans.

Koko is ________. She has had ________—some cats and a bird—over the years. And she often ________ those of humans. Researchers hope to teach her more in the future. And they hope to be able to ________.

Organizer Listen to the talk again. Then, fill in the blanks with the correct words.

Koko the Gorilla
Was born in the San Francisco Zoo in ⓐ ________
Is a western lowland gorilla
Is a part of the Gorilla Foundation
Was taught ASL along with the gorilla ⓑ ________
Knows more than ⓒ ________ signs
Can understand more than ⓓ ________ English words
Has an IQ between 70 and ⓔ ________
Has had cats and ⓕ ________ as pets

12

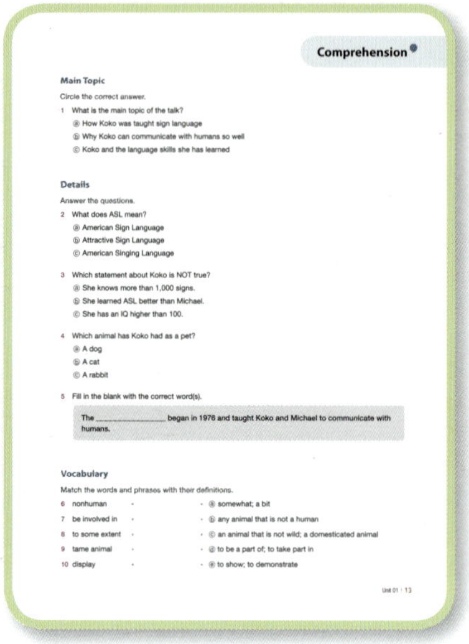
Comprehension

Main Topic

Circle the correct answer.

1 What is the main topic of the talk?
ⓐ How Koko was taught sign language
ⓑ Why Koko can communicate with humans so well
ⓒ Koko and the language skills she has learned

Details

Answer the questions.

2 What does ASL mean?
ⓐ American Sign Language
ⓑ Attractive Sign Language
ⓒ American Singing Language

3 Which statement about Koko is NOT true?
ⓐ She knows more than 1,000 signs.
ⓑ She learned ASL better than Michael.
ⓒ She has an IQ higher than 100.

4 Which animal has Koko had as a pet?
ⓐ A dog
ⓑ A cat
ⓒ A rabbit

5 Fill in the blank with the correct word(s).

The ________________ began in 1976 and taught Koko and Michael to communicate with humans.

Vocabulary

Match the words and phrases with their definitions.

6 nonhuman · · ⓐ somewhat; a bit
7 be involved in · · ⓑ any animal that is not a human
8 to some extent · · ⓒ an animal that is not wild; a domesticated animal
9 tame animal · · ⓓ to be a part of; to take part in
10 display · · ⓔ to show; to demonstrate

Unit 01 13

Comprehension

This page contains several questions about the main talk. There is a question about the main topic or main idea of the talk. There are also four questions that ask about the details in the talk. Finally, there are five vocabulary questions for learners to test their knowledge of the words in the talk.

Listening Skills Practice

This section provides further practice for learners. First, there is a listening skills section in each unit. Various listening skills, such as detail, chronological order, note-taking, dictation, and outlining, are covered in each unit. There is a description of the listening skill as well as questions for learners to test their understanding of the listening skill.

In addition, there is a short talk that is around 150-170 words long. Each talk provides information about a topic related to the main talk. There are comprehension questions and listening skill questions for each short talk as well.

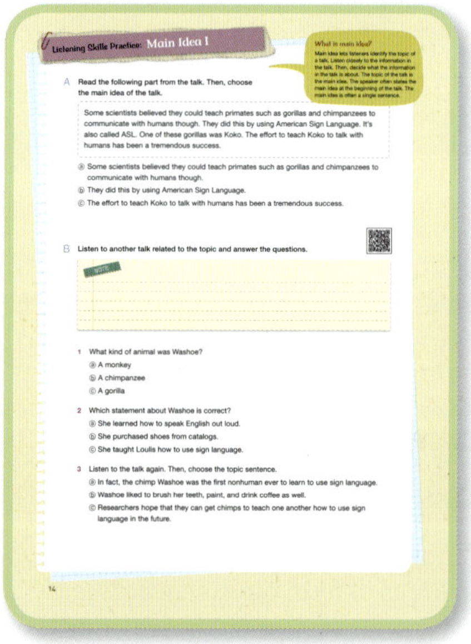
Listening Skills Practice: Main Idea I

A Read the following part from the talk. Then, choose the main idea of the talk.

Some scientists believed they could teach primates such as gorillas and chimpanzees to communicate with humans though. They did this by using American Sign Language. It's also called ASL. One of these gorillas was Koko. The effort to teach Koko to talk with humans has been a tremendous success.

ⓐ Some scientists believed they could teach primates such as gorillas and chimpanzees to communicate with humans though.
ⓑ They did this by using American Sign Language.
ⓒ The effort to teach Koko to talk with humans has been a tremendous success.

B Listen to another talk related to the topic and answer the questions.

1 What kind of animal was Washoe?
ⓐ A monkey
ⓑ A chimpanzee
ⓒ A gorilla

2 Which statement about Washoe is correct?
ⓐ She learned how to speak English out loud.
ⓑ She purchased shoes from catalogs.
ⓒ She taught Loulis how to use sign language.

3 Listen to the talk again. Then, choose the topic sentence.
ⓐ In fact, the chimp Washoe was the first nonhuman ever to learn to use sign language.
ⓑ Washoe liked to brush her teeth, paint, and drink coffee as well.
ⓒ Researchers hope that they can get chimps to teach one another how to use sign language in the future.

14

Chapter

1

Amazing Animals

Unit 01

Koko the Gorilla

Pre-Listening Questions

Answer the following questions.

1 What kind of animal is a gorilla?

2 Have you ever heard of Koko the Gorilla? Why is she famous?

3 How do you think some animals can communicate with humans?

4 Would you like to communicate with animals? Why or why not?

Vocabulary

Write the correct word or phrase from the box for each definition.

primate	handler	communicate	captivity	tremendous	effort

1 ____________ the state of not being free

2 ____________ a group of mammals that includes monkeys, apes, gorillas, and humans

3 ____________ very large; great

4 ____________ to talk; to speak

5 ____________ an attempt

6 ____________ a person who takes care of someone or something else

Koko the Gorilla

Listen to the talk. Fill in the blanks as you listen.

Humans have long wanted to ____________________. They've been able to do this ____________________. For instance, ____________________ such as "Sit," "Come," and "Roll over." ____________________ can understand a small number of instructions. But animals ____________________ in any languages that people can understand.

Some scientists believed ____________________ such as gorillas and chimpanzees ____________________ though. They did this ____________________. It's also called ASL. ____________________ was Koko. The effort to teach Koko to talk with humans has been ____________________.

Koko was born ____________________ in 1971. She has spent ____________________. Koko is a western lowland gorilla. In 1976, the Gorilla Foundation was established. ____________________ two gorillas to communicate with humans by using ASL. Two gorillas were involved in the project: ____________________. Both learned ASL, but ____________________ than Michael.

In fact, Koko has learned more language than ____________________. She is ____________________ although she is rather old for a gorilla. She knows more than 1,000 signs, and she can understand more than ____________________. Her handlers believe her IQ is ____________________. 100 is average for humans.

Koko is ____________________. She has had ____________________—some cats and a bird—over the years. And she often ____________________ those of humans. Researchers hope to teach her more in the future. And they hope to be able to ____________________.

Organizer Listen to the talk again. Then, fill in the blanks with the correct words.

Koko the Gorilla

- Was born in the San Francisco Zoo in ⓐ __________
- Is a western lowland gorilla
- Is a part of the Gorilla Foundation
- Was taught ASL along with the gorilla ⓑ __________

- Knows more than ⓒ __________ signs
- Can understand more than ⓓ __________ English words
- Has an IQ between 70 and ⓔ __________
- Has had cats and ⓕ __________ as pets

Comprehension

Main Topic

Circle the correct answer.

1 What is the main topic of the talk?

ⓐ How Koko was taught sign language

ⓑ Why Koko can communicate with humans so well

ⓒ Koko and the language skills she has learned

Details

Answer the questions.

2 What does ASL mean?

ⓐ American Sign Language

ⓑ Attractive Sign Language

ⓒ American Singing Language

3 Which statement about Koko is NOT true?

ⓐ She knows more than 1,000 signs.

ⓑ She learned ASL better than Michael.

ⓒ She has an IQ higher than 100.

4 Which animal has Koko had as a pet?

ⓐ A dog

ⓑ A cat

ⓒ A rabbit

5 Fill in the blank with the correct word(s).

The ________________ began in 1976 and taught Koko and Michael to communicate with humans.

Vocabulary

Match the words and phrases with their definitions.

6 nonhuman •	• ⓐ somewhat; a bit
7 be involved in •	• ⓑ any animal that is not a human
8 to some extent •	• ⓒ an animal that is not wild; a domesticated animal
9 tame animal •	• ⓓ to be a part of; to take part in
10 display •	• ⓔ to show; to demonstrate

Listening Skills Practice: Main Idea I

What is main idea?

Main idea lets listeners identify the topic of a talk. Listen closely to the information in the talk. Then, decide what the information in the talk is about. The topic of the talk is the main idea. The speaker often states the main idea at the beginning of the talk. The main idea is often a single sentence.

A **Read the following part from the talk. Then, choose the main idea of the talk.**

Some scientists believed they could teach primates such as gorillas and chimpanzees to communicate with humans though. They did this by using American Sign Language. It's also called ASL. One of these gorillas was Koko. The effort to teach Koko to talk with humans has been a tremendous success.

ⓐ Some scientists believed they could teach primates such as gorillas and chimpanzees to communicate with humans though.
ⓑ They did this by using American Sign Language.
ⓒ The effort to teach Koko to talk with humans has been a tremendous success.

B **Listen to another talk related to the topic and answer the questions.**

NOTE

1 What kind of animal was Washoe?
ⓐ A monkey
ⓑ A chimpanzee
ⓒ A gorilla

2 Which statement about Washoe is correct?
ⓐ She learned how to speak English out loud.
ⓑ She purchased shoes from catalogs.
ⓒ She taught Loulis how to use sign language.

3 Listen to the talk again. Then, choose the topic sentence.
ⓐ In fact, the chimp Washoe was the first nonhuman ever to learn to use sign language.
ⓑ Washoe liked to brush her teeth, paint, and drink coffee as well.
ⓒ Researchers hope that they can get chimps to teach one another how to use sign language in the future.

Unit 02

Seeing-Eye Dogs

Pre-Listening Questions

Answer the following questions.

1 What is happening in the picture?

2 What do seeing-eye dogs do?

3 What other animals can help people?

4 How do you feel about service animals? Are they helpful to people?

Vocabulary

Write the correct word or phrase from the box for each definition.

avoid	bond	breed	master	fortunate	assist

1 ____________ an owner; a boss

2 ____________ to help

3 ____________ a type; a kind

4 ____________ to keep from doing something

5 ____________ lucky

6 ____________ a connection; a link

Seeing-Eye Dogs

Listen to the talk. Fill in the blanks as you listen.

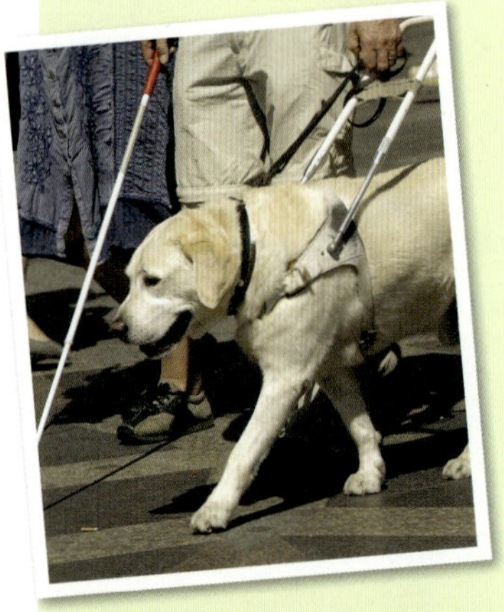

Many blind people have problems going ______________________. When they go outside, they use canes that ______________________ in front of them. This ______________________ people or objects. Nevertheless, for these people, ______________________. Other blind people are ______________________. They have ______________________ that assist them. Blind people with seeing-eye dogs can ______________________.

Seeing-eye dogs are ______________________. They can ______________________ and help them avoid hitting others. They can ______________________. Many of them can even ______________________. Basically, seeing-eye dogs ______________________ of blind people and therefore ______________________.

Many breeds of dogs can become seeing-eye dogs. The first seeing-eye dogs were German shepherds. Golden retrievers and Labrador retrievers are often seeing-eye dogs, too. The dogs must be ______________________. They need to be ______________________ as well. Then, the dogs ______________________. There, dog trainers teach them ______________________. Finally, the dog and its owner are matched. They train together ______________________. That way, they can ______________________.

Seeing-eye dogs and their owners frequently ______________________. The dogs not only lead their owners around but ______________________ their owners' ______________________. In addition, guide dogs are ______________________ around the world. So their owners can take them into lots of business establishments, ______________________. Thus seeing-eye dogs ______________________ of their owners.

Organizer Listen to the talk again. Then, fill in the blanks with the correct words.

How Seeing-Eye Dogs Help

- Are ⓐ ____________ to help people
- Can lead people down streets and help them ⓑ ____________
- Can relieve their owners' feelings of stress and ⓒ ____________
- Act as the ⓓ ____________ of their owners

Seeing-Eye Dogs

- Are German shepherds, golden retrievers, and Labrador retrievers
- Must be big, ⓔ ____________, and in good health
- Train together with their ⓕ ____________
- Are trained at a school

Comprehension

Main Topic

Circle the correct answer.

1 What is the main idea of the talk?

ⓐ Seeing-eye dogs can be various breeds of dogs.

ⓑ Every blind person should have a seeing-eye dog.

ⓒ Seeing-eye dogs are helpful to many blind people.

Details

Answer the questions.

2 What can seeing-eye dogs do for their owners?

ⓐ They can help their owners get onto buses.

ⓑ They can lead their owners down sidewalks.

ⓒ They can assist their owners at their jobs.

3 Which breed of dog is NOT a seeing-eye dog?

ⓐ Bulldog

ⓑ German shepherd

ⓒ Labrador retriever

4 How long do seeing-eye dogs train with their owners?

ⓐ About one month

ⓑ About six months

ⓒ About one year

5 Fill in the blank with the correct word(s).

Seeing-eye dogs are able to reduce the feelings of ________________ and loneliness their masters have.

Vocabulary

Match the words and phrases with their definitions.

6 sidewalk	ⓐ to work; to operate
7 in good health	ⓑ healthy
8 function	ⓒ to hit; to collide with
9 run into	ⓓ to teach
10 train	ⓔ a paved area next to a road that people walk on

Listening Skills Practice: Main Idea II

What is main idea?

Main idea lets listeners identify the topic of a talk. Listen closely to the information in the talk. Then, decide what the speaker is mostly talking about. Many times, the speaker states the main idea in a single sentence. This is the topic sentence. The topic sentence is usually at the beginning of the talk, but it sometimes appears at the end.

A **Read the following part from the talk. Then, choose the main idea of the talk.**

> Seeing-eye dogs and their owners frequently form close bonds. The dogs not only lead their owners around but also help relieve their owners' feelings of stress and loneliness. In addition, guide dogs are becoming more accepted around the world. So their owners can take them into lots of business establishments, including restaurants. Thus seeing-eye dogs greatly improve the quality of life of their owners.

ⓐ Seeing-eye dogs and their owners frequently form close bonds.
ⓑ In addition, guide dogs are becoming more accepted around the world.
ⓒ Thus seeing-eye dogs greatly improve the quality of life of their owners.

B **Listen to a report by a student related to the topic and answer the questions.**

NOTE

1 Where do miniature horses often live?
ⓐ In barns
ⓑ On farms
ⓒ Indoors

2 What can service monkeys do?
ⓐ They can pull wheelchairs.
ⓑ They can answer telephones.
ⓒ They can lead blind people.

3 Listen to the talk again. Then, choose the topic sentence.
ⓐ Most people know about seeing-eye dogs.
ⓑ Two of the more common service animals are miniature horses and monkeys.
ⓒ People who are allergic to dog hair often use them as service animals.

Unit 03

Military Dolphins

Pre-Listening Questions

Answer the following questions.

1 What is the dolphin in the picture doing?

2 How do you think dolphins can help the military?

3 What other animals do you know that the military uses?

4 What is your opinion about the military using animals?

Vocabulary

Write the correct word or phrase from the box for each definition.

researcher	hull	protect	mine	positive	detect

1 ____________ to guard; to watch over

2 ____________ a person who does research

3 ____________ a bomb that is placed in the water and used against ships and submarines

4 ____________ the bottom part of a ship

5 ____________ to find

6 ____________ certain; sure

Military Dolphins

Listen to the talk. Fill in the blanks as you listen.

One night, a terrorist __________. He dives underwater and swims toward a navy base. His objective is __________. He wants to attach a bomb to the ship's hull. Then, it will __________. Suddenly, a dolphin __________. Then, a second dolphin appears. One dolphin stays near the terrorist while __________. A moment later, several navy divers appear. They capture the terrorist and __________ going off. But the real heroes are the dolphins. They found the terrorist.

This might sound like something from __________, but it isn't. __________ are real. The United States Navy has been training dolphins since the 1960s. At first, the U.S. Navy studied dolphins and other sea animals to learn __________. They wanted to make their __________. Then, the researchers realized that they could train the dolphins to __________. So the U.S. Navy captured some dolphins and __________.

The program has been successful. Dolphins are __________. They're among __________ on the planet. I also think they're amazing animals. I love the way that they __________. Anyway, the dolphins learned many skills. The U.S. Navy trained them __________ as well as mines. Mines are bombs that can destroy large ships. The dolphins also learned to __________, to bring items to divers, and to __________. They helped the U.S. Navy in the Vietnam War as well as the first and second Gulf wars. I'm positive dolphins will be useful in the future as well.

Organizer Listen to the talk again. Then, fill in the blanks with the correct words.

Military Dolphins

- ⓐ __________ started studying them in the 1960s
- Wanted to learn how they moved underwater
- Realized they could train the dolphins
- ⓑ __________ some and started training them

- Can detect enemy divers and ⓒ __________
- Can retrieve ⓓ __________
- Can protect ships and ⓔ __________
- Have helped the U.S. Navy in the Vietnam War and both ⓕ __________

Comprehension

Main Topic

Circle the correct answer.

1 What is the main idea of the talk?

ⓐ The U.S. Navy started training dolphins in the 1960s.

ⓑ Dolphins can help the military in a variety of ways.

ⓒ Dolphins have helped the military in several wars.

Details

Answer the questions.

2 What is the terrorist trying to do?

ⓐ Put a bomb on an aircraft carrier

ⓑ Kill the navy divers

ⓒ Attack an army base

3 When did the U.S. Navy start training dolphins?

ⓐ In the 1940s

ⓑ In the 1950s

ⓒ In the 1960s

4 Which war did dolphins NOT help the U.S. Navy in?

ⓐ The Korean War

ⓑ The Vietnam War

ⓒ The First Gulf War

5 Fill in the blank with the correct word(s).

Dolphins are very ________________ animals, so they can be trained to do many activities.

Vocabulary

Match the words and phrases with their definitions.

6	go off	ⓐ a large ship that planes can take off and land from
7	retrieve	ⓑ to cooperate; to act when with others
8	aircraft carrier	ⓒ to recover; to find something and to bring it back
9	scuba gear	ⓓ to explode
10	interact	ⓔ equipment that lets a person breathe underwater

Listening Skills Practice: Fact and Opinion I

What is fact and opinion?

Fact and opinion can separate statements of fact from people's thoughts and feelings. Facts are true statements. They can provide information about people, places, things, or events. Opinions are people's thoughts and feelings about things. Listen carefully so that you can determine which statements are facts and which ones are opinions.

A Read the sentences. Then, write F (fact) or O (opinion).

ⓐ ________ The U.S. Navy captured some dolphins and began training them.

ⓑ ________ I'm positive dolphins will be useful in the future as well.

ⓒ ________ I love the way that dolphins swim and interact with humans.

B Listen to another talk related to the topic and answer the questions.

NOTE

1 Which statement about the California sea lion is true?

ⓐ It can grow very long fur.

ⓑ It weighs up to 3,000 kilograms.

ⓒ It is a playful animal.

2 Which of the following statements is an opinion?

ⓐ One common species is the California sea lion.

ⓑ Personally, I love watching them perform.

ⓒ This is used to guard navy ships that are near shore.

3 Match the sentences to complete the facts.

ⓐ They are trained to swim	ⓘ work together to protect navy ships.
ⓑ Sea lions and humans	ⓘⓘ behind an enemy diver.
ⓒ A rope is attached	ⓘⓘⓘ to the clamp.

Unit 04

Bloodhounds

Pre-Listening Questions

Answer the following questions.

1 What is the dog in the picture doing?

2 What do you think is special about bloodhounds?

3 What are some other types of dogs that you know?

4 How can some dogs help humans?

Vocabulary

Write the correct word or phrase from the box for each definition.

evidence	murderer	relentless	alley	convict	scent

1 ____________ a smell; an odor

2 ____________ proof

3 ____________ determined; never giving up

4 ____________ to declare that a person is guilty of a crime

5 ____________ a person who has killed another human

6 ____________ the small area between two buildings

Bloodhounds

Listen to the talk. Fill in the blanks as you listen.

Last night, a murderer ____________________. Many of ____________________ were worried. They were afraid the police wouldn't catch him. I believed the police would be successful though. The reason is that they ____________________. It only took the bloodhound ____________________ the missing prisoner. He was hiding in an alley ____________________ from the jail. The police recaptured him and took him back to prison. I'm sure ____________________ if they didn't have a bloodhound on the police force.

Bloodhounds are ____________________. They're very powerful and can weigh up to fifty kilograms. They have ____________________, and they make great pets, too. But the best part about them is their noses. They have ____________________. They often ____________________ and try to follow them. So they're ____________________. As a matter of fact, their curiosity can ____________________. Sometimes they smell something new and wander off ____________________ of the scent.

Bloodhounds frequently use their excellent noses to help humans. Many police forces use bloodhounds. Bloodhounds can pick up human scents that are ____________________. When they start tracking a scent, they ____________________. They ____________________. Some bloodhounds have tracked down humans after traveling ____________________. Courts all around the world ____________________. In fact, one bloodhound was so effective that ____________________ more than 600 criminals.

Organizer Listen to the talk again. Then, fill in the blanks with the correct words.

Bloodhounds

- Are powerful and weigh up to ⓐ __________ kilograms
- Have excellent personalities
- Have very ⓑ __________ noses
- Often ⓒ __________ in search of the sources of scents

- Can use their noses to help humans
- Work together with ⓓ __________
- Never give up when ⓔ __________ a scent
- Can help convict ⓕ __________ in court

Main Topic

Circle the correct answer.

1 What is the main topic of the talk?

ⓐ Bloodhounds are excellent at tracking down scents.

ⓑ Every police force should have a bloodhound.

ⓒ Bloodhounds can follow scents better than other dogs.

Details

Answer the questions.

2 How did the police quickly recapture the murderer?

ⓐ By tracking his cell phone

ⓑ By using a bloodhound

ⓒ By finding him on security cameras

3 What is very sensitive on a bloodhound?

ⓐ Its nose

ⓑ Its tail

ⓒ Its eyes

4 Which statement about bloodhounds is NOT correct?

ⓐ They can detect human scents 100 hours old.

ⓑ They do not make very good pets for people.

ⓒ They never give up when they are tracking a scent.

5 Fill in the blank with the correct word(s).

Bloodhounds are so curious that they often wander off when they detect a new ________________.

Vocabulary

Match the words and phrases with their definitions.

6	track down	ⓐ to detect; to locate
7	pick up	ⓑ to walk away from where one is supposed to be
8	recapture	ⓒ to find someone or something after searching for a while
9	wander off	ⓓ to catch someone a second time
10	jail	ⓔ a prison; a place where criminals are kept

Listening Skills Practice: Fact and Opinion II

What is fact and opinion?

Fact and opinion can separate statements of fact from people's thoughts and feelings. Facts are all of the details in a talk. They are true statements about people, places, things, or events. In talks, people frequently give their opinions about facts. They may use the words *think*, *believe*, and *feel* when they state their opinions.

A **Read the sentences. Then, write F (fact) or O (opinion).**

ⓐ ________ Bloodhounds are my favorite breed of dog.

ⓑ ________ The police recaptured him and took him back to prison.

ⓒ ________ Some bloodhounds have tracked down humans after traveling more than 160 kilometers.

B **Listen to a newscaster give a report related to the topic and answer the questions.**

Memo

1 What did Friday do?

ⓐ He took a bomb apart.

ⓑ He detected a bomb.

ⓒ He caught a terrorist.

2 Which of the following statements is an opinion?

ⓐ Authorities have just announced they stopped a terrorist plot to destroy an airplane.

ⓑ Fortunately, the airport has a number of bomb-detection dogs.

ⓒ We'll have more on this breaking news story in just a few minutes.

3 Match the sentences to complete the facts.

ⓐ The bomb was	ⓘ big enough to destroy the plane.
ⓑ Friday sniffed	ⓘⓘ bomb squad arrived.
ⓒ Members of the	ⓘⓘⓘ something strange in the bag.

Chapter

2

Famous Journeys

Unit 05

Ferdinand Magellan

Pre-Listening Questions

Answer the following questions.

1 Who was Ferdinand Magellan? What did he do?

2 What do you think it would be like to sail on the ship in the picture?

3 Have you ever sailed on a ship? How was it?

4 What kind of journey would you like to take? Why?

Vocabulary

Write the correct word or phrase from the box for each definition.

funds	mutiny	execute	native	reject	passageway

1 ____________ to rebel against one's leader

2 ____________ a way through a place

3 ____________ a person who lives in a certain place

4 ____________ money

5 ____________ to turn down; to say no to

6 ____________ to put someone to death for committing a crime

Ferdinand Magellan

Listen to the talk. Fill in the blanks as you listen.

After Christopher Columbus __________ in 1492, many Europeans __________. One of these men was Ferdinand Magellan. Magellan was born in Portugal in 1480. As a young man, he __________. But he did that __________. Magellan believed he could get to India faster __________. He asked the king of Portugal for funds. But the king rejected Magellan. Magellan then asked King Charles V of Spain for assistance. Charles agreed, so Magellan __________.

In September 1519, more than 270 men __________. First, they sailed to the Canary Islands. They're in the middle of the Atlantic Ocean. Then, they __________. The ships sailed far to the south __________. The ships __________. So some of the crew mutinied. But Magellan __________ of the mutiny.

Finally, Magellan __________ around the tip of South America. This place is called the Strait of Magellan. The water in this ocean __________. Magellan decided to __________. After four months of sailing, three of Magellan's ships arrived at the Mariana Islands. Then, the ships __________. Magellan's crew __________ there though. Around forty men—and Magellan himself—__________.

__________ to return to Spain. They finished their journey __________. Only one ship and __________ the trip. They became the first men ever to __________.

Organizer Listen to the talk again. Then, fill in the blanks with the correct words.

Ferdinand Magellan

- Visited India by going around ⓐ __________
- Wanted to travel ⓑ __________ to get to Asia
- Request for funds was rejected by the king of ⓒ __________
- Was given funds by the king of Spain

- Traveled south around the tip of South America
- Went across ⓓ __________ to the Mariana Islands
- Was killed by natives in ⓔ __________
- ⓕ __________ sailors returned to Spain and sailed around the world

Comprehension

Main Topic

Circle the correct answer.

1 What is the main topic of the talk?

ⓐ The dangers of traveling to islands in the Pacific Ocean

ⓑ The life and adventures of Magellan

ⓒ The journey around the world by Magellan and his crew

Details

Answer the questions.

2 Who provided Magellan with funds to travel across the Atlantic Ocean?

ⓐ King Charles V of Spain

ⓑ The king of Portugal

ⓒ Christopher Columbus

3 Where is the Strait of Magellan?

ⓐ By the Canary Islands

ⓑ Near the coast of Spain

ⓒ At the tip of South America

4 What did NOT happen during Magellan's journey?

ⓐ Magellan was killed by natives in the Philippines.

ⓑ All five of Magellan's ships returned to Spain.

ⓒ Some of the crew mutinied against Magellan.

5 Fill in the blank with the correct word(s).

The first trip around the world began in ________________ and ended in 1522.

Vocabulary

Match the words and phrases with their definitions.

6 agree •	• ⓐ the top or end of something
7 survivor •	• ⓑ to say yes to something; to decide to do something
8 journey •	• ⓒ to use all of something, such as supplies
9 tip •	• ⓓ a person who lives through an event
10 run out of •	• ⓔ a long trip

Listening Skills Practice: Sequencing I

What is sequencing?

Sequencing involves putting the events in a talk in the correct order. Listen carefully to the talk to make sure you hear the order of events properly. The speakers will sometimes provide days, months, years, and dates. They can help you get the events in the correct order.

A Listen to the talk again. Then, put the sentences in the correct order.

ⓐ ________ Some of Magellan's crew mutinied, but Magellan defeated them.

ⓑ ________ Magellan and around forty of his men were killed in a fight.

ⓒ ________ Three of Magellan's ships arrived in the Mariana Islands.

B Listen to another talk related to the topic and answer the questions.

NOTE

1 What was a problem with traveling through the Strait of Magellan?

ⓐ They were difficult to find.

ⓑ The water in them was rough.

ⓒ The water in them was shallow.

2 Which country did Verrazano sail for?

ⓐ France

ⓑ Italy

ⓒ England

3 Put the following sentences in the correct order.

ⓐ ________ Verrazano sailed into New York Bay and met some Native Americans.

ⓑ ________ Verrazano sailed around South Carolina.

ⓒ ________ Verrazano headed north and went to Newfoundland.

Unit 06

Roald Amundsen

Pre-Listening Questions

Answer the following questions.

1 Who was Roald Amundsen?

2 What can you see in the picture to the right?

3 How would you like to visit Antarctica?

4 What do you think it would be like to go there?

Vocabulary

Write the correct word or phrase from the box for each definition.

trek	adventurous	tragic	expedition	airship	desire

1 ____________ a long and difficult trip

2 ____________ very sad or unfortunate

3 ____________ a strong urge or feeling; a want

4 ____________ a mission

5 ____________ brave; daring; feeling like doing something dangerous

6 ____________ a blimp; a lighter-than-air ship

Roald Amundsen

Listen to the talk. Fill in the blanks as you listen.

Some men ____________ and rarely leave their hometowns. Others are ____________. Roald Amundsen was ____________. Born in Norway in 1872, Amundsen ____________ of the world.

Amundsen's first great adventure began ____________. He was searching for ____________. Ever since the Europeans discovered the Americas, they had sought the Northwest Passage. ____________ from the Atlantic Ocean to the Pacific Ocean ____________. Many men tried to find it. Yet ____________. Amundsen, however, found it during a journey that ____________.

Later, in 1910, Amundsen ____________ the South Pole and sailed to Antarctica. ____________, his ship arrived in Antarctica. His team ____________. Then, on October 14, 1911, five men, fifty-two dogs, and four sleds began the trek to the bottom of the Earth. It was a difficult journey, but, ____________, they made it. They were ____________ a British expedition led by Robert Scott. ____________ the return trip to their ship. Sadly, ____________ survived.

Amundsen had ____________ the North Pole as well. In 1926, he ____________ an Italian and an American. They ____________ the North Pole. As they flew above it, all three men ____________ onto the North Pole. Two years later, Amundsen's life ____________. He was on a rescue mission ____________. Only pieces of the plane were found. Amundsen's body ____________.

Organizer Listen to the talk again. Then, fill in the blanks with the correct words.

Antarctica

- Arrived on ⓐ __________, 1911, and began preparing
- ⓑ __________ men, fifty-two dogs, and four sleds left
- Was faster than a ⓒ __________ expedition led by Robert Scott
- Arrived at the South Pole on ⓓ __________, 1911

The North Pole

- Teamed up with an ⓔ __________ and an American
- Flew over the North Pole in an airship
- Dropped flags over ⓕ __________

Comprehension

Main Topic

Circle the correct answer.

1 What is the main idea of the talk?

ⓐ Roald Amundsen made a visit to the South Pole.

ⓑ Roald Amundsen traveled widely in the polar regions.

ⓒ Roald Amundsen died in a tragic plane crash.

Details

Answer the questions.

2 What was Roald Amundsen's first great adventure?

ⓐ He went to the South Pole.

ⓑ He found the Northwest Passage.

ⓒ He visited the North Pole.

3 Which is NOT true about Roald Amundsen's trip to Antarctica?

ⓐ He and Robert Scott went to the South Pole together.

ⓑ He used dogs and sleds to get to the South Pole.

ⓒ He became the first man to go to the South Pole.

4 How did Roald Amundsen go to the North Pole?

ⓐ By sled

ⓑ By plane

ⓒ By airship

5 Fill in the blank with the correct word(s).

Roald Amundsen disappeared while on a ________________ mission, and his body was never found.

Vocabulary

Match the words and phrases with their definitions.

6 team up with •	• ⓐ the second of two
7 polar region •	• ⓑ the place where a person was born or grew up
8 latter •	• ⓒ to work together with someone
9 set one's sights on •	• ⓓ a very cold area near the North Pole or South Pole
10 hometown •	• ⓔ to make a goal; to have an objective

Listening Skills Practice: Sequencing II

What is sequencing?

Sequencing involves putting the events in a talk in the correct order. Start with the first event. Then, put all of the events in the order in which they happened according to the speaker. Speakers often use sequencing words. Some common sequencing words are *first*, *next*, *then*, *after that*, and *last*.

A Listen to the talk again. Then, put the sentences in the correct order.

ⓐ ________ Roald Amundsen led a team of men and dogs to the South Pole.

ⓑ ________ Roald Amundsen was in a plane crash while on a rescue mission.

ⓒ ________ Roald Amundsen spent three years looking for the Northwest Passage.

B Listen to a student give a report related to the topic and answer the questions.

NOTE

1 Who was the first man who claimed to have visited the North Pole?

ⓐ Robert Peary

ⓑ Richard Byrd

ⓒ Frederick Cook

2 How did Richard Byrd say that he had gotten to the North Pole?

ⓐ By flying

ⓑ By using a sled

ⓒ By walking

3 Put the following sentences in the correct order.

ⓐ ________ Robert Peary claimed that he visited the North Pole.

ⓑ ________ Roald Amundsen and two others went to the North Pole.

ⓒ ________ Richard Byrd said that he had flown over the North Pole.

Unit 07

Captain Cook

Pre-Listening Questions

Answer the following questions.

1 What did Captain Cook do?

2 When did Captain Cook live?

3 What famous sailors in history do you know?

4 How would you like to take a cruise on the ocean?

Vocabulary

Write the correct word or phrase from the box for each definition.

rumor	confirm	enlist	apprentice	head	superior

1 ____________ to go toward

2 ____________ to prove that something is true

3 ____________ a boss; a manager; someone in a higher position

4 ____________ a person who learns a skill from another

5 ____________ gossip; a story about a person or thing that may or may not be true

6 ____________ to join the military

Captain Cook

Listen to the talk. Fill in the blanks as you listen.

James Cook was born __________________. While he grew up on a farm, Cook had __________________. Instead, he __________________. After he turned eighteen, he went to sea __________________ on a merchant ship. Then, when the French and Indian War began, he __________________.

Cook loved maps and __________________. While he was in the Royal Navy, __________________ his mapmaking skills. Those skills __________________ of a ship. In 1768, he departed for the South Pacific Ocean on his first great expedition. During his trip, he visited Tahiti. He mapped most of __________________ of New Zealand. And he visited __________________. When he returned home, __________________.

In 1772, Cook __________________ his second expedition. It lasted until 1775. Cook had __________________ a continent south of Australia. He __________________ his expedition further south than anyone had sailed before. However, the weather was cold, and __________________ in the water, so the ships __________________. Cook was __________________ of land south of Australia.

In 1776, Cook went on __________________. He was searching for __________________. He __________________ but could not find a way into the Atlantic Ocean. Then, Cook and his crew headed south, where they __________________. Unfortunately, Cook's men and the islanders __________________. One of the Hawaiians killed Cook and __________________ one of England's greatest adventurers.

Organizer Listen to the talk again. Then, fill in the blanks with the correct words.

Captain Cook

- Sailed in the South Pacific for ⓐ __________ years
  - Visited Tahiti and eastern Australia
  - Mapped most of the 2 main islands of ⓑ __________
- Sailed from 1772 to 1775
  - Was looking for a continent south of ⓒ __________
  - Had to turn back because of ⓓ __________ and ice
- Started searching for the Northwest Passage in ⓔ __________
  - Went to Alaska and then to ⓕ __________
  - Was killed by an islander in 1779

Comprehension

Main Topic

Circle the correct answer.

1 What is the main topic of the talk?

ⓐ The three expeditions of Captain Cook

ⓑ The military career of Captain Cook

ⓒ The battles that Captain Cook fought

Details

Answer the questions.

2 Where did Captain Cook NOT visit on his first expedition?

ⓐ Tahiti

ⓑ New Zealand

ⓒ Hawaii

3 What was the purpose of Captain Cook's second expedition?

ⓐ To find the Northwest Passage

ⓑ To map the coast of New Zealand

ⓒ To find a southern continent

4 What happened to Captain Cook on his third expedition?

ⓐ An islander killed him.

ⓑ He became an admiral.

ⓒ He found Antarctica.

5 Fill in the blank with the correct word(s).

Captain Cook went on three different expeditions while serving in the ________________.

Vocabulary

Match the words and phrases with their definitions.

6 agriculture •	• ⓐ a ship that carries good to sell
7 end the life of •	• ⓑ farming
8 merchant ship •	• ⓒ a person who lives on an island
9 be fascinated by •	• ⓓ to kill
10 islander •	• ⓔ to be interested in; to be amazed by

Listening Skills Practice: Word Stress I

What is word stress?

Word stress happens when a speaker emphasizes the important words or phrases in a sentence. Speakers stress words by speaking them a little more strongly than the other words. That way, the listeners will recognize that the words are important. Do not use word stress too often. Use it only for the most important words.

A Listen to the talk again. Then, circle the words that the speaker stresses.

ⓐ Cook loved maps and was good at drawing them.

ⓑ When he returned home, three years had passed.

ⓒ He sailed up to Alaska but could not find a way into the Atlantic Ocean.

B Listen to another talk related to the topic and answer the questions.

NOTE

1 Who discovered the Mississippi River?

ⓐ The English

ⓑ The French

ⓒ The Spanish

2 What did Marquette and Joliet do?

ⓐ They sailed to the source of the Mississippi River.

ⓑ They canoed down a large part of the Mississippi River.

ⓒ They fought some Spaniards along the Mississippi River.

3 Listen to the talk again. Then, circle the words that the speaker stresses.

ⓐ The greatest river in North America is the Mississippi River.

ⓑ At that point, the two men then realized that the river flowed into the Gulf of Mexico.

ⓒ Not wanting to fight the Spanish, they turned around and returned to the north.

Unit 08

Stanley and Livingstone

Pre-Listening Questions

Answer the following questions.

1 What is happening in the picture?

2 Who were Stanley and Livingstone?

3 Why did people call Africa "the Dark Continent" in the past?

4 Where in Africa would you like to visit? Why?

Vocabulary

Write the correct word or phrase from the box for each definition.

dense	missionary	disaster	inhospitable	presume	porter

1 ____________ a person who carries another person's luggage

2 ____________ a person who tries to convert others to his or her religion

3 ____________ thick

4 ____________ unfriendly; difficult to be or live in

5 ____________ to assume; to believe to be true

6 ____________ a terrible event; a tragedy

Stanley and Livingstone

Listen to the talk. Fill in the blanks as you listen.

For centuries, people called Africa "____________________." Even though ____________________, the Europeans ____________________ from the coast. Much of the northern part of Africa ____________________. And the middle part is ____________________. It wasn't until the 1800s that the Europeans ____________________ of the continent.

Dr. David Livingstone was ____________________. He first went to Africa ____________________. He spent many years there and ____________________ around the continent. During his time there, he traveled through much of the interior. He ____________________. And he was one of the first people to ____________________. Then, in 1866, Dr. Livingstone went on a journey to find ____________________. Unfortunately, it was a disaster. His porters deserted him. ____________________ were stolen. And Livingstone ____________________.

Back in Europe, ____________________ Dr. Livingstone for a few years. People ____________________. So the *New York Herald*, an American newspaper, sent Henry Morgan Stanley to Africa. His goal was to ____________________. In 1871, Stanley started in Zanzibar. He had more than 200 porters and ____________________. Stanley's journey was ____________________ Livingstone's. His porters deserted him. Others ____________________ on a journey that covered more than 1,000 kilometers.

Finally, ____________________, Stanley entered Ujiji, a village in Tanzania. He saw ____________________ Africans and Arabs. He then ____________________, "Dr. Livingstone, I presume?" The man simply answered, "Yes."

Organizer Listen to the talk again. Then, fill in the blanks with the correct words.

Dr. Livingstone

- Was a Scottish missionary who went to Africa
- Discovered ⓐ __________
- Started looking for the ⓑ __________ of the Nile River
- ⓒ __________ somewhere in Africa

Henry Morgan Stanley

- Went to Africa to find ⓓ __________
- Had a ⓔ __________ journey.
- Went to the village of ⓕ __________
- Saw a white man and said, "Dr. Livingstone, I presume?"

Comprehension

Main Topic

Circle the correct answer.

1 What is the main idea of the talk?

ⓐ Dr. Livingstone lived and traveled in Africa for many years.

ⓑ Stanley managed to find Dr. Livingstone in Africa.

ⓒ Most people called Africa "the Dark Continent."

Details

Answer the questions.

2 What is the northern part of Africa like?

ⓐ Desert

ⓑ Jungle

ⓒ Plains

3 What did Dr. Livingstone NOT do in Africa?

ⓐ He looked for the source of the Nile River.

ⓑ He mapped the interior of Africa.

ⓒ He discovered Victoria Falls.

4 What did Stanley say to Dr. Livingstone?

ⓐ Dr. Livingstone, I presume?

ⓑ Dr. Livingstone, is that you?

ⓒ Dr. Livingstone, where have you been?

5 Fill in the blank with the correct word(s).

Stanley searched for Dr. Livingstone because an American ________________ sent him to Africa.

Vocabulary

Match the words and phrases with their definitions.

6 transcontinental journey •	• ⓐ being all around
7 utter •	• ⓑ the inside of something
8 interior •	• ⓒ to say; to speak
9 surrounded by •	• ⓓ to leave someone alone
10 desert •	• ⓔ a trip from one side of a continent to the other

Listening Skills Practice: Word Stress II

What is word stress?

Word stress happens when a speaker emphasizes the important words or phrases in a sentence. By stressing these words, the speakers indicate their importance. Speakers often stress words such as *not*, *very*, *really*, *always*, and *never*. They also often stress numbers and dates.

A Listen to the talk again. Then, circle the words that the speaker stresses.

ⓐ And Livingstone became very sick.

ⓑ Back in Europe, no one heard from Dr. Livingstone for a few years.

ⓒ Stanley's journey was almost as bad as Livingstone's.

B Listen to a talk by a newscaster related to the topic and answer the questions.

Memo

1 How did Hendri Coetzee die?

ⓐ His boat sank.

ⓑ He went over a waterfall.

ⓒ A crocodile killed him.

2 What did Hendri Coetzee and his crew do?

ⓐ They discovered the source of the Lukuga River.

ⓑ They sailed from the source of the Nile River to the end.

ⓒ They sailed their ship over a waterfall in the Nile River.

3 Listen to the talk again. Then, circle the words that the speaker stresses.

ⓐ Today, December 10, 2010, one of the great travelers of African rivers was lost.

ⓑ An adventuresome person, he also enjoyed going over waterfalls in boats.

ⓒ They were the first people ever to sail the entire length of the Nile River from its beginning to its end.

Chapter

3

American Folklore

Unit 09

Pocahontas

Pre-Listening Questions

Answer the following questions.

1 What can you see in the picture?

2 Who was Pocahontas? What do you know about her?

3 Do you know the names of any famous American Indians?

4 How would you feel if people tried to colonize your country? Why would you feel that way?

Vocabulary

Write the correct word or phrase from the box for each definition.

celebrity	convert	establish	permanent	clash	club

1 ____________ to found; to start

2 ____________ a famous person

3 ____________ a large stick that one uses as a weapon

4 ____________ to change from one religion to another; to change one's thoughts

5 ____________ to fight

6 ____________ forever; not ending; long lasting

Pocahontas

Listen to the talk. Fill in the blanks as you listen.

In 1607, the English ______________________ in North America. The site was Jamestown, Virginia. There were ______________________, and their leader was ______________________.

The colonists landed in a place ______________________. Many ______________________ the colonists. They had met other Englishmen before, and those men ______________________. So the Indians ______________________ the new colonists. As a result, the two sides often ______________________.

______________________, the members of a tribe captured John Smith. They took him to Powhatan. He was ______________________. Powhatan ______________________. Some members of the tribe put Smith's head ______________________. They prepared to ______________________. Then, Pocahontas, one of Powhatan's daughters, went to Smith and ______________________. In that way, she ______________________.

Pocahontas ______________________. In 1609, most of the colonists died ______________________. But Pocahontas helped the colonists ______________________. She warned them when some Indians were going to attack, too. Thanks to her, the colonists were prepared, so ______________________.

In 1612, the colonists captured Pocahontas ______________________. During her time ______________________, she converted to Christianity. She also ______________________ John Rolfe, one of the colonists. The two got married and ______________________. There, ______________________. While in England, she became sick though. She and her husband ______________________, but Pocahontas ______________________ and never returned to her homeland.

Organizer Listen to the talk again. Then, fill in the blanks with the correct words.

John Smith

- Was the ⓐ __________ of the English colonists at Jamestown
- Was captured and brought to ⓑ __________
- Was ⓒ __________ when Pocahontas put her head on his
- Was about to be executed

Pocahontas

- Was friends with the ⓓ __________
- Provided the colonists with food and help
- Went to England but ⓔ __________ and died there
- Converted to ⓕ __________ and married John Rolfe

Comprehension

Main Topic

Circle the correct answer.

1 What is the main topic of the talk?

ⓐ The lives of Pocahontas and Powhatan

ⓑ Pocahontas and her relationship with the English

ⓒ John Smith the English colony of Jamestown

Details

Answer the questions.

2 Who was Powhatan?

ⓐ An English colonist

ⓑ The leader of an Indian tribe

ⓒ John Smith's Indian guide

3 What is NOT true about Pocahontas?

ⓐ She saved the life of John Smith.

ⓑ She gave help to the English colonists.

ⓒ She led an attack against Jamestown.

4 Where did Pocahontas die?

ⓐ In England

ⓑ In America

ⓒ In France

5 Fill in the blank with the correct word(s).

Pocahontas converted to Christianity, and then she ________________ John Rolfe.

Vocabulary

Match the words and phrases with their definitions.

6	hostile	ⓐ to kill
7	captivity	ⓑ unfriendly
8	execute	ⓒ to hit a person so many times that he or she dies
9	beat to death	ⓓ a condition in which one has been captured
10	harsh	ⓔ difficult; cruel

Listening Skills Practice: Dictation I

What is dictation?

Dictation is writing down words exactly as a person says them. In some cases, you need to write down every word in a sentence. Use dictation to do this. By practicing dictation, you can improve your listening skills. You can make your spelling and punctuation better. And you can learn to write faster, too.

A **Listen to the talk again. Practice dictation by writing the exact words the speaker says.**

ⓐ On one occasion, ______________________________.

ⓑ In 1609, ______________________________.

ⓒ The two got married and ______________________________.

B **Listen to another talk related to the topic and answer the questions.**

NOTE

1 What was the name of Sacajawea's tribe?

ⓐ The Hopi

ⓑ The Sioux

ⓒ The Shoshone

2 What did Sacajawea do for the Lewis and Clark expedition?

ⓐ She worked as a translator.

ⓑ She served as a guide.

ⓒ She helped fight other Indians.

3 Listen to the talk again. Practice dictation by writing the exact words the speaker says.

ⓐ Their goal was to ______________________________.

ⓑ Fortunately, a woman named Sacajawea ______________________________.

ⓒ She helped to negotiate trades for ______________________________.

Unit 10

Johnny Appleseed

Pre-Listening Questions

Answer the following questions.

1 What is happening in the picture on the left?

2 What do you think Johnny Appleseed did?

3 What do you think it would be like to live in a land with few people?

4 Would you like to live in a land with few people? Why or why not?

Vocabulary

Write the correct word or phrase from the box for each definition.

serve	folklore	orchard	frontier	settler	inland

1 ____________ away from an ocean or sea

2 ____________ a group of fruit or nut trees

3 ____________ land that is far away from places where most people live

4 ____________ a legend; a myth; a story from the past that may or may not be true

5 ____________ to do a job; to have a position

6 ____________ a person who is among the first to move to a new region to live

Johnny Appleseed

Listen to the talk. Fill in the blanks as you listen.

The ______________ the states of Ohio, Indiana, and Illinois. Many people don't think of them ______________. However, in the 1700s and part of the 1800s, they were ______________. The reason is that the early American colonies were all ______________. So few people ever ______________.

The people who did travel ______________ of America were ______________. They ______________. And they ______________. Johnny Appleseed was one of these people.

______________ was John Chapman. He was born in Massachusetts in 1774. When he was young, he ______________ in an orchard. There, he ______________. At the age of eighteen, he left Massachusetts and ______________. First, he lived in western Pennsylvania. He ______________. He didn't simply plant trees anywhere though. Instead, he planted ______________ and took care of them for a year or two. Then, as settlers arrived in the area, he ______________.

Thanks to ______________, people called him Johnny Appleseed. Johnny soon left Pennsylvania and ______________ Ohio. He traveled all around Ohio and planted numerous apple trees. Johnny had ______________. He lived simply, too. He wore ______________ and a cooking pot for a hat. The Indians who saw him ______________. Even when they were fighting settlers, they ______________. Today, Johnny Appleseed is one of the most famous figures ______________.

Organizer Listen to the talk again. Then, fill in the blanks with the correct words.

Johnny Appleseed

- Was an apprentice at an ⓐ __________
- Moved west to ⓑ __________
- Planted groups of apple trees and took care of them
- Sold the trees to ⓒ __________ who arrived
- Moved to ⓓ __________ and planted many trees
- Wore cloth sacks for clothes and a cooking pot for a hat
- Was respected by ⓔ __________
- Is a ⓕ __________ from American folklore

Comprehension

Main Topic

Circle the correct answer.

1 What is the main idea of the talk?

ⓐ Johnny Appleseed was a colorful American folk hero.

ⓑ Johnny Appleseed moved to the west as a young man.

ⓒ Johnny Appleseed planted more trees than any other man.

Details

Answer the questions.

2 Which state is NOT in the American Midwest?

ⓐ Ohio

ⓑ Indiana

ⓒ Massachusetts

3 What did Johnny Appleseed do with the apple trees he planted?

ⓐ He gave them away.

ⓑ He sold them.

ⓒ He chopped them down.

4 How did the Indians feel about Johnny Appleseed?

ⓐ They respected him.

ⓑ They disliked him.

ⓒ They thought of him as a brother.

5 Fill in the blank with the correct word(s).

Johnny Appleseed wore cloth sacks for clothes and put a ________________ on his head for a hat.

Vocabulary

Match the words and phrases with their definitions.

6 figure •	• ⓐ a sack that is made from cloth
7 colorful character •	• ⓑ an entertaining or amusing person
8 respect •	• ⓒ to look after; to care for
9 take care of •	• ⓓ a person; an individual
10 cloth sack •	• ⓔ to think highly of another person

Listening Skills Practice: Dictation II

What is dictation?

Dictation is writing down the words exactly as a person says them. You may need to write down all of the words a person says because they are all important. Use your dictation skills to do this. Focus on the speaker's words and try to remember all of them. Then, write them down in the same order that the speaker says them.

A **Listen to the talk again. Practice dictation by writing the exact words the speaker says.**

ⓐ However, in the 1700s and part of the 1800s, ____________________.

ⓑ When he was young, ____________________.

ⓒ The Indians who saw him ____________________.

B **Listen to a report by a student related to the topic and answer the questions.**

NOTE

1 What does a lumberjack do?

ⓐ Cuts down trees

ⓑ Farms the land

ⓒ Catches fish

2 According to legends, what did Paul Bunyan NOT create?

ⓐ The Great Lakes

ⓑ The Grand Canyon

ⓒ Yellowstone National Park

3 Listen to the talk again. Practice dictation by writing the exact words the speaker says.

ⓐ Paul Bunyan is my ____________________.

ⓑ Even as a baby, ____________________.

ⓒ He and Babe were walking one day, and Paul ____________________.

Unit 11 The First Thanksgiving

Pre-Listening Questions

Answer the following questions.

1 What are the people in the picture doing?

2 What do you know about American Thanksgiving?

3 Is there a holiday like Thanksgiving in your country? What is the name of the holiday?

4 How do the people in your country celebrate that holiday?

Vocabulary

Write the correct word or phrase from the box for each definition.

harmful	beneficial	harvest	sap	feast	store

1 ____________ dangerous

2 ____________ the crops that are taken from a field

3 ____________ to save; to put away to use later

4 ____________ a thick liquid that is found in trees

5 ____________ helpful

6 ____________ an event in which a lot of food is served

The First Thanksgiving

Listen to the talk. Fill in the blanks as you listen.

In 1620, ____________ called the Pilgrims ____________ the *Mayflower*. There were 110 Pilgrims. They ____________ and arrived in America on November 10. They landed in Plymouth ____________ the Massachusetts Bay Colony.

Their first winter in Massachusetts ____________. ____________ survived the cold, snowy winter weather. The next year in March, ____________ their camp. He looked at them and said, "Welcome." The Pilgrims were surprised ____________. His name was Samoset. He and another Indian, Squanto, ____________. They showed the Pilgrims ____________ and other crops. They taught the Pilgrims how to get sap from maple trees. And they showed the Pilgrims ____________ and which ones were beneficial.

That fall, the Pilgrims ____________. They had plenty of food to eat and ____________ for the winter. They had ____________ and meat. The Pilgrims had built a large number of homes and other buildings as well. They decided to celebrate ____________. They ____________. They invited Samoset, Squanto, and many other Indians. Around ____________ for the event. ____________, the Pilgrims and Indians celebrated. They ate food and ____________. That was the first Thanksgiving in America.

Today, Thanksgiving is ____________. Americans celebrate it ____________ of November every year. It's one of the most important holidays in the country.

Organizer Listen to the talk again. Then, fill in the blanks with the correct words.

The Pilgrims

- Landed in ⓐ __________, Massachusetts after sailing on the *Mayflower*
- Most ⓑ __________ during the first harsh winter
- Learned how to plant crops from the Indians
- Were helped by the Indians ⓒ __________ and Squanto

The First Thanksgiving

- Had a good ⓓ __________ and lots of food as well as many buildings
- Invited Samoset, Squanto, and other Indians
- ⓔ __________ food and played many games
- Celebrated for ⓕ __________

Comprehension

Main Topic

Circle the correct answer.

1 What is the main idea of the talk?

ⓐ The Pilgrims made friends with Samoset and Squanto.

ⓑ The Pilgrims had a difficult time when they moved to America.

ⓒ The Pilgrims celebrated the first Thanksgiving in America.

Details

Answer the questions.

2 What did Samoset say to the Pilgrims when he met them?

ⓐ Hello.

ⓑ Good morning.

ⓒ Welcome.

3 How did Samoset and Squanto NOT assist the Pilgrims?

ⓐ They showed them how to plant crops.

ⓑ They showed them how to fish in the ocean.

ⓒ They showed them how to get sap from trees.

4 How long did the first Thanksgiving celebration last?

ⓐ 1 day

ⓑ 2 days

ⓒ 3 days

5 Fill in the blank with the correct word(s).

The Pilgrims sailed on the ________________ and landed at Plymouth, Massachusetts.

Vocabulary

Match the words and phrases with their definitions.

6 show up •	• ⓐ to depart on a ship
7 set sail •	• ⓑ to appear
8 national holiday •	• ⓒ a variety of; many types of
9 all kinds of •	• ⓓ to have a good time at a special event
10 celebrate •	• ⓔ a special day that everyone in a country enjoys

Listening Skills Practice: Guessing Unknown Words I

What is guessing unknown words?

Guessing unknown words is a way to learn what the difficult words in a talk mean. Listen carefully when the speaker uses difficult words. Many times, the speaker will provide clues in the talk. These clues can help you guess the meanings of the difficult words.

A **Guess the meaning of the underlined word.**

Their first winter in Massachusetts was <u>dreadful</u>. Fewer than fifty Pilgrims survived the cold, snowy winter weather.

ⓐ long
ⓑ terrible
ⓒ shocking

B **Listen to another talk related to the topic and answer the questions.**

NOTE

1 Which place did Squanto NOT visit?
ⓐ England
ⓑ Spain
ⓒ Germany

2 What happened to many of the members of Squanto's tribe?
ⓐ The Pilgrims killed them.
ⓑ They died from smallpox.
ⓒ They moved to another place.

3 Guess the meaning of the underlined word.

He also provided lots of <u>assistance</u> for them. Without Squanto, the Pilgrims might not have survived the first year.

ⓐ gifts
ⓑ advice
ⓒ help

Unit 12

Davy Crockett

Pre-Listening Questions

Answer the following questions.

1 How would you describe the man in the picture?

2 What kind of a man do you think Davy Crockett was?

3 What do you know about life on the American frontier?

4 What was life like in your country two centuries ago? How did people live then?

Vocabulary

Write the correct word or phrase from the box for each definition.

wild	reputation	cattle	territory	represent	scout

1 ____________ land

2 ____________ a soldier who moves ahead of the main group in order to look for danger

3 ____________ how people think or feel about another person

4 ____________ untamed; uncivilized

5 ____________ to act and speak for another person or a group of people

6 ____________ cows

Davy Crockett

Listen to the talk. Fill in the blanks as you listen.

In the ____________________, lots of Americans began moving west. They ____________________ such as Ohio, Indiana, Kentucky, and Tennessee. These lands ____________________. But many people didn't ____________________.

In 1786, Davy Crockett was born to a family that ____________________ in Tennessee. He ____________________ and was driving cattle to Virginia when he ____________________. Crockett's father ____________________ though, so he ran away from home as a young boy. He lived in Virginia for a while and got married. But he ____________________ Tennessee.

In Tennessee, he began to ____________________ as a frontiersman. He served in the military to ____________________. As a soldier, he ____________________. He was also ____________________. People easily recognized him by ____________________ on his head.

Crockett realized that the people living on the frontier ____________________. So he decided to represent them. He ____________________. First, he served in the Tennessee legislature. Later, he ____________________ in the U.S. Congress. He served in the House of Representatives.

In 1836, he ____________________, so he left Washington, D.C. He and his family then moved to Texas. Texas had just ____________________. In response, ____________________ parts of Texas. Crockett went to the Alamo in San Antonio, Texas. The Mexican army ____________________ and attacked. Crockett died at the Alamo on ____________________. After his death, people began telling a number of legends and ____________________.

Organizer Listen to the talk again. Then, fill in the blanks with the correct words.

Davy Crockett

- Was born on the frontier in Tennessee
- Worked hard as a boy and was treated badly by ⓐ ____________
- ⓑ ____________ from home and got married
- Moved back to Tennessee with his family

- ⓒ ____________ in the military as a scout
- Acted as a ⓓ ____________ for people living on the frontier
- Served in ⓔ ____________
- Went to ⓕ ____________ and was killed by Mexicans at the Alamo

Comprehension

Main Topic

Circle the correct answer.

1 What is the main topic of the talk?

ⓐ Davy Crockett's time in the military

ⓑ Davy Crockett and his time in Texas

ⓒ The life of Davy Crockett

Details

Answer the questions.

2 What did Davy Crockett do as a young boy?

ⓐ He ran away from home.

ⓑ He moved to Texas.

ⓒ He joined the military.

3 What did Davy Crockett do in the military?

ⓐ He was a general.

ⓑ He was a scout.

ⓒ He was a sailor.

4 Which of the following is NOT true about Davy Crockett?

ⓐ He got involved in politics.

ⓑ He lived most of his life in Washington, D.C.

ⓒ He took his family to Texas.

5 Fill in the blank with the correct word(s).

Davy Crockett went to Texas, but he was killed at the ________________ when the Mexican army attacked it.

Vocabulary

Match the words and phrases with their definitions.

6	coonskin cap	ⓐ a person who lives in the wild
7	legislature	ⓑ to treat badly; to act tough toward
8	frontiersman	ⓒ a hat made from the skin of a raccoon
9	spokesperson	ⓓ a person who speaks for others
10	be hard on	ⓔ a group of representatives that makes laws

Listening Skills Practice: Guessing Unknown Words II

What is guessing unknown words?

Guessing unknown words is a way to learn what the difficult words in a talk mean. Pay close attention to the context of a talk. In other words, be aware of what the speaker is talking about. If you understand the context, then you can figure out the meanings of all of the difficult words.

A **Guess the meaning of the underlined word.**

Texas had just declared its independence from Mexico. In response, Mexican soldiers <u>invaded</u> parts of Texas.

ⓐ attacked

ⓑ shot at

ⓒ avoided

B **Listen to a talk by a tour guide related to the topic and answer the questions.**

Memo

1 Who was Santa Anna?

ⓐ The leader of the Texans at the Alamo

ⓑ The leader of the Texan army

ⓒ The leader of the Mexican army

2 Who did NOT die at the Alamo?

ⓐ Jim Bowie

ⓑ Sam Houston

ⓒ William Travis

3 Guess the meaning of the underlined word.

When Texas declared its independence, the Mexicans were <u>displeased</u>. So they sent an army into Texas.

ⓐ unhappy

ⓑ unaware

ⓒ uncivilized

Chapter

4

Historical Mysteries

Unit 13

The Lost Colony of Roanoke

Pre-Listening Questions

Answer the following questions.

1 What can you see in the picture?

2 How could a colony become lost?

3 Would it be easy or difficult to live in a colony? Why do you think so?

4 Would you like to live in a foreign land? Why or why not?

Vocabulary

Write the correct word or phrase from the box for each definition.

nobody	establish	plant	colonize	carve	governor

1 ____________ to cut with a knife

2 ____________ to start a colony

3 ____________ to put seeds into the ground in the hope that they will grow

4 ____________ no person; no one

5 ____________ the leader of a colony or state

6 ____________ to start; to found; to create

The Lost Colony of Roanoke

Listen to the talk. Fill in the blanks as you listen.

In 1607, some men and women successfully established ____________________ in North America. The name of the colony was Jamestown. Jamestown wasn't the first English attempt ____________________ in North America though. ____________________, some people tried to found a colony south of Jamestown. ____________________ was Roanoke Island.

Roanoke Island ____________________ of the American state of North Carolina. In 1585, a group of Englishmen ____________________ a colony there. Sadly, they didn't ____________________. And founding the colony was too hard for them. So they ____________________ and sailed back to England. Strangely, the soldiers ____________________, and nobody ever saw them again.

Two years later, in 1587, ____________________ arrived. They saw ____________________ of the first colony on Roanoke Island. That sight ____________________. Unfortunately, they ____________________ in the year ____________________. Yet there was some good news. On August 15, 1587, Virginia Dare was born. She was ____________________ born in North America.

A few days later, John White, the governor of the colony, left. He returned to England ____________________. He wanted to return quickly. But he didn't go back to Roanoke ____________________. When he arrived, ____________________. There weren't even any bodies. White searched carefully. All he found was ____________________: CROATAN. It was the name of ____________________. But the colonists weren't there. To this day, ____________________ to the lost colony of Roanoke.

Organizer Listen to the talk again. Then, fill in the blanks with the correct words.

The Lost Colony of Roanoke

- Was located off the coast of ⓐ __________
- Was an early attempt by the English to found a colony
- First attempt was in ⓑ __________
- Colonists gave up and ⓒ __________ to England

- Made another attempt in ⓓ __________
- Governor ⓔ __________ went back to England for more supplies
- Returned 3 years later, but the entire colony was gone
- Only found the word ⓕ __________ carved in a tree

Comprehension

Main Topic

Circle the correct answer.

1 What is the main topic of the talk?

ⓐ Some reasons that the colony of Roanoke may have disappeared

ⓑ The founding and disappearance of the colony of Roanoke

ⓒ The difficulties the colonists had in founding the colony of Roanoke

Details

Answer the questions.

2 What did the first colonists who went to Roanoke Island do?

ⓐ They gave up and went back to England.

ⓑ They moved to the colony of Jamestown.

ⓒ They all died while fighting the Indians.

3 Who was Virginia Dare?

ⓐ The governor of the colony of Roanoke

ⓑ A member of a tribe of Indians near Roanoke

ⓒ The first English baby born in North America

4 Which of the following statements is NOT true?

ⓐ John White did not return to Roanoke for three years.

ⓑ John White found the word CROATAN carved in a year.

ⓒ John White found some colonists living with an Indian tribe.

5 Fill in the blank with the correct word(s).

Roanoke was an early attempt by the English to found a colony, but the colony failed because everyone ________________.

Vocabulary

Match the words and phrases with their definitions.

6 to this day •	• ⓐ to try
7 get along with •	• ⓑ to return
8 go back •	• ⓒ to have a good relationship with; to be friends with
9 attempt •	• ⓓ the destroyed remains of a building or other structure
10 ruins •	• ⓔ until now; up to the current time

Listening Skills Practice: Paraphrasing I

What is paraphrasing?

Paraphrasing is a way to simplify a long talk. When you are taking notes, you often cannot write down every word the speaker says. Instead, learn to paraphrase. Omit the unimportant words and information. Focus only on the important information. You can often make a single sentence that contains all of the important information from a part of a talk.

A **Read a part of the talk. Then, choose the correct paraphrase.**

> In 1585, a group of Englishmen attempted to start a colony there. Sadly, they didn't get along well with the natives. And founding the colony was too hard for them. So they left a group of soldiers behind and sailed back to England.

ⓐ Only the soldiers were successful while the rest of the colonists went back to England.

ⓑ The Englishmen founded a colony thanks to the soldiers that they brought with them.

ⓒ The Englishmen tried to found a colony, but they gave up and returned home.

B **Listen to another talk related to the topic and answer the questions.**

NOTE

1 Where do many historians think that the lost Roman legion went?

ⓐ To Turkey

ⓑ To China

ⓒ To Russia

2 What have archaeologists found in Zhelaizhai?

ⓐ Roman ruins

ⓑ Roman coins

ⓒ Roman weapons

3 Read a part of the talk. Then, choose the correct paraphrase.

> A Chinese general wrote about a strange practice some of the soldiers they had captured had. They fought in rows and covered one another with their shields. That was a common Roman method of fighting.

ⓐ Some of the soldiers captured by the Chinese had fought like Romans.

ⓑ The Chinese confirmed they had captured some Roman soldiers.

ⓒ The Romans defeated the Chinese by using Roman methods of fighting.

Unit
14
Amelia Earhart

Pre-Listening Questions

Answer the following questions.

1 What do you know about Amelia Earhart?

2 What do you think it would be like to fly in an airplane like the one in the picture?

3 How safe do you think those planes were?

4 Have you ever been lost before? How did you feel?

Vocabulary

Write the correct word or phrase from the box for each definition.

relatively	flight	crash	navigator	impressed	accomplish

1 ____________ fairly; somewhat

2 ____________ a person who manages the course of a vehicle

3 ____________ a trip in the air, often on an airplane

4 ____________ amazed; very interested

5 ____________ to wreck; to have an accident in some kind of a vehicle

6 ____________ to do something successfully

Amelia Earhart

Listen to the talk. Fill in the blanks as you listen.

In 1908, ____________ named Amelia Earhart saw her first airplane. She ____________. More than a decade later in 1920, Amelia ____________ in California. There, she ____________. From then on, flying became her life.

At that time, ____________. Amelia worked hard, saved money, and bought her first plane. She ____________. She became ____________ to fly more than 14,000 feet above the ground. That's more than 4,200 meters high. In 1928, she became the first woman ____________. She wasn't the only one on the plane, so it wasn't a solo flight. It wasn't until 1932 that she ____________ the Atlantic. She was ____________ after Charles Lindbergh to accomplish that feat.

Earhart wasn't satisfied, so she decided to fly ____________. She planned to do this with Fred Noonan, ____________. She started in Miami, Florida, ____________. She made it across Africa and Asia. Then, she arrived in New Guinea. That's ____________. On July 2, Earhart and Noonan took off. Nobody ____________.

There are ____________ what happened. Most people believe her plane ____________. Some say ____________ Earhart and Noonan and then ____________. Others think they ____________ and lived there until they died. And a few individuals even claim that aliens in UFOs abducted them. ____________: Nobody knows exactly what happened to the two of them.

Organizer Listen to the talk again. Then, fill in the blanks with the correct words.

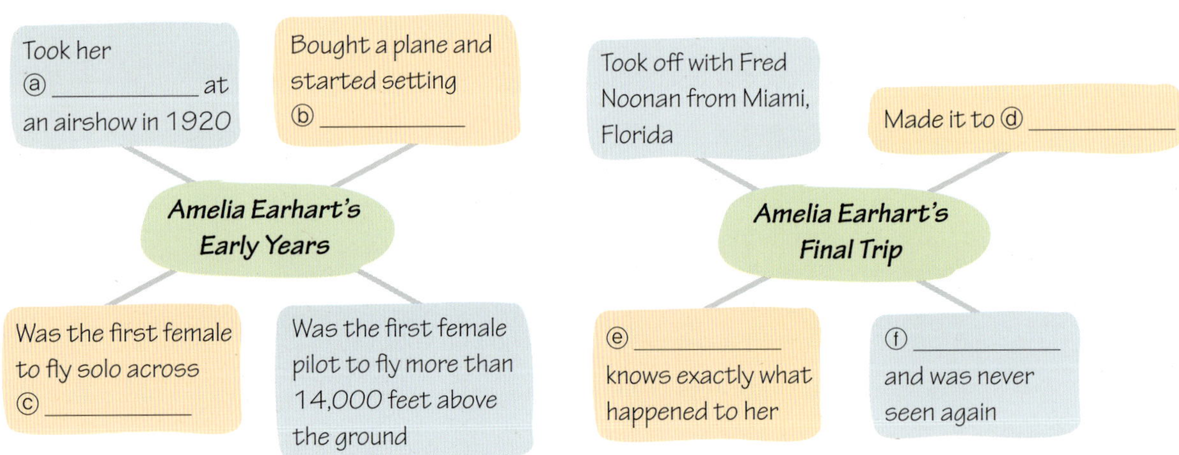

Comprehension

Main Topic

Circle the correct answer.

1 What is the main idea of the talk?

ⓐ Amelia Earhart still might be alive somewhere today.

ⓑ Amelia Earhart was the world's greatest female pilot.

ⓒ Amelia Earhart disappeared on her trip around the world.

Details

Answer the questions.

2 How did Amelia Earhart feel when she saw her first airplane?

ⓐ She fell in love with flying.

ⓑ She thought it looked fun.

ⓒ She was not impressed.

3 Which of the following did Amelia Earhart NOT do?

ⓐ Become the first woman to fly more than 14,000 feet above the ground

ⓑ Become the first woman to fly around the world

ⓒ Become the first woman to fly solo across the Atlantic Ocean

4 Where did Amelia Earhart and Fred Noonan disappear?

ⓐ Near Miami

ⓑ Near New Guinea

ⓒ Near Japan

5 Fill in the blank with the correct word(s).

There are many ________________ about what happened to Amelia Earhart, but no one knows the truth for sure.

Vocabulary

Match the words and phrases with their definitions.

6	spy	ⓐ an island that no one lives on
7	feat	ⓑ a period of ten years
8	desert island	ⓒ an accomplishment; an act; a deed
9	decade	ⓓ an event that features vehicles that can fly
10	airshow	ⓔ a secret agent

Listening Skills Practice: Paraphrasing II

What is paraphrasing?

Paraphrasing is a way to simplify a long talk. You do not need to write down everything the speaker says. Instead, listen to a few sentences, and then make one sentence from them. This sentence should contain a summary and should contain the important facts that the speaker mentions.

A **Read a part of the talk. Then, choose the correct paraphrase.**

> Some say the Japanese captured Earhart and Noonan and then executed them for being American spies. Others think they landed on a desert island and lived there until they died. And a few individuals even claim that aliens in UFOs abducted them. One thing is certain: Nobody knows exactly what happened to the two of them.

ⓐ It is highly likely that the Japanese executed Earhart and Noonan for being spies.

ⓑ People have various ideas about what happened, but no one is sure of the truth.

ⓒ There are not many people who believe that aliens abducted the two.

B **Listen to a talk by a newscaster related to the topic and answer the questions.**

NOTE

1 What do most people know Antoine de Saint-Exupery for?

ⓐ Writing a children's book

ⓑ Serving as a pilot

ⓒ Disappearing one night

2 What did the diver find in the 1980s?

ⓐ An old bracelet

ⓑ A crashed plane

ⓒ A sunken ship

3 Read a part of the talk. Then, choose the correct paraphrase.

> On this day, April 7, 2004, experts now know for sure that they have located Saint-Exupery's plane. The number on the body of the wrecked plane matches that of the plane Saint-Exupery was flying when he disappeared. His body wasn't recovered though. So what happened to it is still a mystery.

ⓐ Saint-Exupery's plane has been found, but his body has not.

ⓑ The plane Saint-Exupery was flying was discovered on April 7, 2004.

ⓒ Authorities believe that Saint-Exupery's plane crashed into the water.

Unit 15

Atlantis

Pre-Listening Questions

Answer the following questions.

1 What was Atlantis?

2 Where was it?

3 How was it destroyed?

4 Do you think that Atlantis actually existed? Why or why not?

Vocabulary

Write the correct word or phrase from the box for each definition.

civilization	tsunami	vast	destruction	simply	philosopher

1 ____________ very large; huge

2 ____________ an advanced culture

3 ____________ a person who thinks deeply about life, ethics, logic, or other similar topics

4 ____________ ruin; damage

5 ____________ a large, fast-moving wave often caused by an earthquake

6 ____________ just; only

Atlantis

Listen to the talk. Fill in the blanks as you listen.

More than 10,000 years ago, there was ____________________ in the Atlantic Ocean. Each of its founders ____________________. The people of the island built ships and had a powerful navy. The island itself had ____________________, silver, and other precious metals. There were ____________________, too. ____________________ was a great capital city. This was Atlantis. It was the greatest civilization in the ancient world. Then, one day, the people of Atlantis did something to upset the gods. So the gods ____________________. In a single night, the island ____________________.

The Greek philosopher Plato ____________________ in two works ____________________. Since then, others have added to the story. But ____________________ about Atlantis is this: ____________________? No one is sure of the answer.

Many people claim Atlantis ____________________. For instance, some believe it ____________________. They say that it sank when a volcano on the island of Thera erupted around 1500 B.C. That eruption, people believe, ____________________. Others think Atlantis was in the Atlantic Ocean. They believe it was ____________________ Bimini Island off the coast of Florida, USA. But lots of people think Plato ____________________. They ____________________. They also point out that no one has ever found ____________________.

Nevertheless, people ____________________ the lost land. ____________________ they will find proof of the existence of Atlantis someday.

Organizer Listen to the talk again. Then, fill in the blanks with the correct words.

Atlantis

- Was in the Atlantic Ocean
- Was the greatest ⓐ __________ in the ancient world
- Sank one night because its people ⓑ __________ the gods
- Was described by Plato in ⓒ __________ works of his

- ⓓ __________ is sure if Atlantis really existed
- May have been an island in the ⓔ __________
- Are other suggestions as to where it was
- Is not any ⓕ __________ that it ever existed

Comprehension

Main Topic

Circle the correct answer.

1 What is the main idea of the talk?

ⓐ Atlantis may have been a great civilization from the past.

ⓑ It is most likely that Atlantis was in the Atlantic Ocean.

ⓒ The story of Atlantis was told by the philosopher Plato.

Details

Answer the questions.

2 According to the talk, which statement about Atlantis is true?

ⓐ Its founders were regular people.

ⓑ It had a lot of gold and silver.

ⓒ Its people had advanced technology.

3 What did Plato do?

ⓐ He lived in Atlantis.

ⓑ He wrote about Atlantis.

ⓒ He visited Atlantis.

4 Which place is NOT a possible location of Atlantis?

ⓐ Near Bimini Island

ⓑ The coast of Spain

ⓒ The island of Thera

5 Fill in the blank with the correct word(s).

Atlantis was the greatest ________________ in ancient times, but it might not actually have existed.

Vocabulary

Match the words and phrases with their definitions.

6 exist •	• ⓐ to show; to state; to mention
7 make up •	• ⓑ evidence; a fact
8 point out •	• ⓒ to be
9 proof •	• ⓓ a rare animal or one that does not commonly live in a place
10 exotic animal •	• ⓔ to create from one's mind

Listening Skills Practice: Supporting Details I

What are supporting details?
Supporting details can provide extra information. The speaker always has a main point. Then, the speaker provides information about this main point. This information is called the supporting details. Usually, the speaker uses words such as *for example*, *in addition*, *also*, and *such as* when providing supporting details.

A Fill in the blanks with the words from the box.

also	too	for instance

ⓐ The island itself had a vast amount of gold, silver, and other precious metals. There were many exotic animals living there, ____________.

ⓑ Many people claim Atlantis actually existed. ____________, some believe it was located in the Mediterranean Sea.

ⓒ They claim that Atlantis is a myth. They ____________ point out that no one has ever found any evidence Atlantis existed.

B Listen to another talk related to the topic and answer the questions.

NOTE

1 What is the official name of Area 51?
ⓐ Las Vegas
ⓑ Alien City
ⓒ Groom Lake

2 What is a theory about Area 51 that some people believe?
ⓐ There is a spaceport for aliens in it.
ⓑ The U.S. military tests weapons there.
ⓒ The U.S. launches spaceships there.

3 Match the sentences to complete the supporting details.

ⓐ But most people	ⓘ only recently confirmed that the place exists.
ⓑ In addition, others believe scientists	ⓘⓘ know it as Area 51.
ⓒ In fact, the United States government	ⓘⓘⓘ there do research concerning aliens.

Unit 16

The Bermuda Triangle

Pre-Listening Questions

Answer the following questions.

1 What do you think the Bermuda Triangle is?

2 Have you ever been near the Bermuda Triangle? What is it like there?

3 Why do ships and airplanes suddenly disappear?

4 Are there any mysterious places in your country? What makes them mysterious?

Vocabulary

Write the correct word or phrase from the box for each definition.

determine	graveyard	wreckage	fear	instance	vanish

1 ____________ to figure out

2 ____________ to be afraid; to be scared

3 ____________ to disappear

4 ____________ a place where dead people are buried

5 ____________ an event; an example

6 ____________ the remains of a vehicle that has had an accident

The Bermuda Triangle

Listen to the talk. Fill in the blanks as you listen.

Draw a line from __________________ to Bermuda. Then, __________________ from Bermuda to Puerto Rico and one going back to Florida. That __________________. It's known as the Bermuda Triangle or the Devil's Triangle. __________________ going there. The reason is that, in around five centuries, __________________ have disappeared in the Bermuda Triangle.

Sometimes __________________. But people can __________________ the ships sank and why the planes crashed. In the Bermuda Triangle though, ships __________________. Planes also __________________. In most cases, no wreckage is found either. It's like the ships and planes simply disappeared __________________.

For example, in 1918, the *U.S.S. Cyclops* __________________ of 309 people. Somewhere in the Bermuda Triangle, it __________________. Decades later, one of the most famous events involving the Bermuda Triangle occurred. __________________, Flight 19 took off from a naval base in Florida. There were five Avenger bombers in the group. They __________________ in clear weather. In the middle of the flight, __________________ was lost. Nothing was ever heard from any of the men on the planes again. Nor __________________. That same night, two airplanes __________________ the missing planes. One of those planes disappeared.

There have been __________________. No one knows what makes the Bermuda Triangle __________________. That makes it one of the most mysterious places on the Earth.

Organizer Listen to the talk again. Then, fill in the blanks with the correct words.

The Bermuda Triangle

- Is between the southern tip of ⓐ __________, Bermuda, and Puerto Rico
- Is ⓑ __________ by sailors and airmen
- ⓒ __________ ships and planes have disappeared there
- Is a graveyard for ships and planes

- *U.S.S. Cyclops* disappeared there in ⓓ __________
- ⓔ __________ disappeared there in 1945
- One ⓕ __________ disappeared, too
- Have been numerous strange instances there

Comprehension

Main Topic

Circle the correct answer.

1 What is the main topic of the talk?
ⓐ The location of the Bermuda Triangle
ⓑ The mystery of the Bermuda Triangle
ⓒ Some ships that survived the Bermuda Triangle

Details

Answer the questions.

2 Which place is NOT connected to the Bermuda Triangle?
ⓐ Cuba
ⓑ Florida
ⓒ Puerto Rico

3 What happened to the *U.S.S. Cyclops*?
ⓐ It crashed into the ocean.
ⓑ It disappeared without a trace.
ⓒ It was attacked by pirates.

4 Which statement about Flight 19 is correct?
ⓐ The planes were on a bombing mission.
ⓑ The planes were attacked by enemy fighters.
ⓒ The planes suddenly lost radio contact.

5 Fill in the blank with the correct word(s).

The Bermuda Triangle is a ______________ for ships and planes since so many of them vanish there.

Vocabulary

Match the words and phrases with their definitions.

6	clear weather	ⓐ an enclosed object with three sides
7	crash	ⓑ with no evidence
8	triangle	ⓒ to wreck; to run into something
9	naval base	ⓓ weather that is sunny with no clouds in the sky
10	without a trace	ⓔ a place where many navy ships are

Listening Skills Practice: Supporting Details II

What are supporting details?

Supporting details can provide extra information. Every talk has a main point. Supporting details can help support the main point of the talk. They can do this by providing examples as well as giving definitions. A speaker typically gives several supporting examples to make the main point stronger.

A **Write MI (main idea) or SD (supporting detail).**

ⓐ ________ Somewhere in the Bermuda Triangle, the ship vanished without a trace.

ⓑ ________ One of the rescue planes disappeared.

ⓒ ________ In the Bermuda Triangle though, ships often suddenly sink in clear weather.

B **Listen to a report by a student related to the topic and answer the questions.**

NOTE

1 Who was on board the Mary Celeste when the other ship found it?

ⓐ The captain

ⓑ The crew

ⓒ No one

2 What happened to the crew of the *Mary Celeste*?

ⓐ They drowned in the ocean.

ⓑ They got on board another ship.

ⓒ Nobody knows for sure.

3 Fill in the blanks to complete the supporting details.

ⓐ Another ship ____________ the *Mary Celeste*.

ⓑ The ship's cargo and the crew members' ____________ were still on board.

ⓒ It is possible that ____________ killed the crew.

Chapter

5

Music

Unit 17

Louis Armstrong

Pre-Listening Questions

Answer the following questions.

1 What instrument is the man playing?

2 What do you know about Louis Armstrong?

3 What different musical genres are there?

4 Which musical genres do you prefer? Why?

Vocabulary

Write the correct word or phrase from the box for each definition.

distinct	quartet	obvious	hit	cornet	popularize

1 ____________ a success

2 ____________ unique; individual

3 ____________ to make liked or famous

4 ____________ clear

5 ____________ a brass instrument similar to a trumpet

6 ____________ a group of four people

Louis Armstrong

Listen to the talk. Fill in the blanks as you listen.

Louis Armstrong had one of ____________________ in all music. Today, most people ____________________ *What a Wonderful World*. He actually recorded that song ____________________. And it didn't even become a hit ____________________ Armstrong died. ____________________ people don't know more about Armstrong than that one song.

Louis Armstrong was born in New Orleans, Louisiana, in 1901. New Orleans is often called "____________________." The musical tradition in New Orleans ____________________. When he was only eleven years old, he ____________________. He started playing music with a quartet of boys. They sang ____________________ and ____________________.

Armstrong soon learned to play the cornet. It's ____________________ the trumpet. He became an amazing cornet player. Armstrong soon ____________________ other than New Orleans. He played ____________________ the Mississippi River. He went to Chicago and New York City as well. ____________________ to everyone who saw him play.

One time in Chicago, Louis was recording a song. He suddenly ____________________. Instead of stopping, Louis ____________________. But he didn't sing the words. He just ____________________. This was known as scat singing. Armstrong ____________________. During his life, he became very famous. He recorded many hit songs, and he performed almost ____________________. Today, while he isn't as well-known as he once was, ____________________ one of the great musicians of the twentieth century.

Organizer Listen to the talk again. Then, fill in the blanks with the correct words.

Louis Armstrong

- Was born in ⓐ __________, Louisiana
- Played music with a ⓑ __________ of boys
- Learned to play the ⓒ __________
- Performed in many different places

- Dropped the ⓓ __________ while recording once
- Kept ⓔ __________ but made up sounds
- Was doing ⓕ __________ singing
- Made that type of singing popular

Comprehension

Main Topic

Circle the correct answer.

1 What is the main topic of the talk?

ⓐ The childhood of Louis Armstrong

ⓑ The most famous songs of Louis Armstrong

ⓒ The musical career of Louis Armstrong

Details

Answer the questions.

2 Which statement about *What a Wonderful World* is true?

ⓐ It was Louis Armstrong's first hit song.

ⓑ It was recorded early in Louis Armstrong's life.

ⓒ It became popular after Louis Armstrong died.

3 What musical instrument did Louis Armstrong play?

ⓐ The drums

ⓑ The cornet

ⓒ The clarinet

4 What is NOT correct about scat singing?

ⓐ A singer needs a lyric sheet to do it.

ⓑ It consists of sounds that are not words.

ⓒ Louis Armstrong made it popular.

5 Fill in the blank with the correct word(s).

Louis Armstrong was born in New Orleans, which is called "the ____________ of jazz."

Vocabulary

Match the words and phrases with their definitions.

6 drop out of •	• ⓐ the place where a person is born
7 unfortunate •	• ⓑ to quit an activity such as school
8 lyric sheet •	• ⓒ a piece of paper with the words to a song on it
9 scat singing •	• ⓓ sad; unlucky
10 birthplace •	• ⓔ the act of singing syllables that are not really words

Listening Skills Practice: Outlining I

What is outlining?

Outlining is a way to summarize the main points of a talk. Make an outline to focus on the main details of a talk. First, write down the main idea. Then, write down a few details that describe the main idea. When you make your outline, do not use sentences. Instead, use short phrases and words.

A Listen to the talk again. Then, complete the outline by using the words in the box.

performed	lyric sheet	quartet	tradition	cornet

Louis Armstrong

I. Was born in New Orleans, Louisiana
  i. Was influenced by the musical ⓐ __________ there
  ii. Dropped out of school when he was eleven
  iii. Sang with a ⓑ __________ of boys

II. Learned to play the ⓒ __________
  i. Was an amazing player
  ii. ⓓ __________ in places other than New Orleans
  iii. Played in Chicago and New York

III. Popularized scat singing
  i. Dropped the ⓔ __________ but kept singing
  ii. Didn't sing words but made up sounds

B Listen to another talk related to the topic and answer the questions.

NOTE

1 Complete the outline by filling in the blanks.

Ella Fitzgerald

I. Was a ⓐ __________ musician

II. Had a successful singing career
  i. Sold ⓑ __________ of albums
  ii. Won numerous awards
  iii. Was called "the ⓒ __________ of jazz" and "the first lady of song"
  iv. Had an incredible voice

III. Sang many ⓓ __________
  i. Mostly performed jazz music
  ii. Played bebop, soul, ⓔ __________, and the blues
  iii. Was an accomplished scat musician
  iv. Sang solo and played with others

Unit 18

George Frideric Handel

Pre-Listening Questions

Answer the following questions.

1. What can you see in the picture on the right?
2. Who was George Frideric Handel?
3. What else do you know about him?
4. How do you like classical music? Why do you feel that way?

Vocabulary

Write the correct word or phrase from the box for each definition.

barge	act	request	harpsichord	patron	conduct

1. ____________ a keyboard instrument that is related to the piano
2. ____________ to perform in front of others
3. ____________ a large, flat boat used to carry cargo on rivers
4. ____________ a person who provides funds for an artist to do work
5. ____________ to lead a group of musicians
6. ____________ to ask someone to do something

George Frideric Handel

Listen to the talk. Fill in the blanks as you listen.

George Frideric Handel was born ____________________. His father wanted him ____________________. Handel was more interested in music though. As a child, he ____________________. He learned to play the harpsichord, violin, oboe, and organ. And he learned ____________________. Despite ____________________, Handel began studying law. A year later, his father died, so Handel ____________________ and began focusing on music.

His true love was Italian opera, so he ____________________ about it. Then, in 1710, Prince George of Hanover ____________________. In 1714, Prince George would become King George I of England. By that time, Handel himself ____________________. He ____________________, so he composed music, ____________________, for them.

It was in England that Handel wrote his greatest pieces of music. In 1717, he ____________________ for the first time. ____________________ in the middle of the Thames River as King George I himself watched. The king loved the music so much that he requested to ____________________.

Years later, in 1741, Handel ____________________ *The Messiah*. It was an oratorio. An oratorio is a musical piece that often ____________________. An orchestra performs, and there are ____________________, but the singers don't act like ____________________. Handel wrote ____________________ in his life. *The Messiah* ____________________ and most popular of them all. On April 14, 1759, a few days ____________________ of *The Messiah*, Handel died.

Organizer Listen to the talk again. Then, fill in the blanks with the correct words.

Early Life

- ⓐ __________ wanted him to be a lawyer
- Learned to compose music and to play ⓑ __________
- Focused on music after his father ⓒ __________
- Studied law despite have musical talent

Life in England

- Had many ⓓ __________, so composed music for them
- Conducted *Water Music* for King George I
- Wrote many ⓔ __________ during his life
- Finished ⓕ __________ in 1741

Comprehension

Main Topic

Circle the correct answer.

1 What is the main idea of the talk?

ⓐ *The Messiah* was the greatest oratorio that Handel ever wrote.

ⓑ Handel went against his father's wishes and became a musician.

ⓒ Handel became a successful composer of many types of music.

Details

Answer the questions.

2 Which musical instrument did Handel NOT play?

ⓐ The oboe

ⓑ The violin

ⓒ The clarinet

3 What did King George I think of *Water Music*?

ⓐ He asked to hear it again several times.

ⓑ He thought it was Handel's best music.

ⓒ He never wanted to hear it again.

4 What kind of work is *The Messiah*?

ⓐ An opera

ⓑ An oratorio

ⓒ A symphony

5 Fill in the blank with the correct word(s).

Handel's father wanted him to become a ________________, but he was much more interested in music.

Vocabulary

Match the words and phrases with their definitions.

6 compose •	• ⓐ a woodwind instrument that has a double reed
7 rank as •	• ⓑ a piece of music that is sung by a chorus
8 oboe •	• ⓒ to write or create a work of art
9 apparent •	• ⓓ clear; obvious
10 choral work •	• ⓔ to have a standing

Listening Skills Practice: Outlining II

What is outlining?

Outlining is a way to summarize the main points of a talk. It helps provide order by listing the main idea of a talk with some details beneath each main idea. When making an outline, just use the important information. Do not include the minor points and details. By using outlines, you can understand the information in a talk much better.

A Listen to the talk again. Then, complete the outline by using the words in the box.

requested	lessons	operas	greatest	England

George Frideric Handel

I. Was interested in music as a child
   i. Took music ⓐ ____________
   ii. Learned to play the harpsichord, violin, oboe, and organ
   iii. Learned to compose music
II. Moved to ⓑ ____________
   i. Had many patrons
   iii. Composed music such as ⓒ ____________ for them
III. Some famous works
   i. Conducted *Water Music* for King George I in 1717
   ii. King liked so much that he ⓓ ____________ to hear it several times
   iii. Finished the oratorio *The Messiah* in 1741
   iv. Is the ⓔ ____________ and most popular of all of Handel's oratorios

B Listen to a talk by an usher related to the topic and answer the questions.

Memo

1 Complete the outline by filling in the blanks.

The Messiah

I. Was composed by Handel in 1740
II. Tells the story of the life, ⓐ ____________, and resurrection of Jesus Christ
III. Creation of *The Messiah*
   i. Words taken from the ⓑ ____________
   ii. Took ⓒ ____________ days to compose the music
IV. *Hallelujah* chorus
   i. Is the most recognizable piece
   ii. King George II was ⓓ ____________ by the chorus
   iii. ⓔ ____________ in the middle of it, so everyone else stood
   iv. Audiences around the world stand for it today

Unit 19

Renaissance Musical Instruments

Pre-Listening Questions

Answer the following questions.

1 What are the names of the musical instruments in the pictures?

2 What kinds of musical instruments are they?

3 What are some other musical instruments people played during the Renaissance?

4 Which of the musical instruments in the pictures would you like to play? Why?

Vocabulary

Write the correct word or phrase from the box for each definition.

strum	emphasize	evolve	funeral	bow	resemble

1 ____________ a long stick used to play some musical instruments

2 ____________ a ceremony held when a person dies

3 ____________ to touch the strings of a musical instrument such as a guitar

4 ____________ to look like; to appear to be

5 ____________ to stress

6 ____________ to change over a long period of time

Renaissance Musical Instruments

Listen to the talk. Fill in the blanks as you listen.

The Renaissance began around 1400 and __________. There were __________ during it. People focused on __________. They also __________. During the Renaissance, people played __________. Some of these instruments later evolved into the modern ones that people play today.

__________ were very popular at that time. The lute was probably the most common of them. It __________. In fact, the guitar evolved from the vihuela, a Spanish lute. A person played the lute __________ with his or her fingers. The viol and rebec were two other stringed instruments that people played then. To make music with them, the musicians __________. The modern-day violin developed from the rebec. Finally, the hurdy-gurdy was __________. It looked like a violin, but it also __________.

__________ are among the oldest of all musical instruments. So it's no surprise that people played them during the Renaissance. The recorder, __________, was played by many musicians. People played the recorder __________ and funerals. __________, which later became the modern flute, was another woodwind from that time.

Brass instruments such as the trumpet and trombone __________. Instead, some people played the sackbut. Like the trombone, __________ that musicians could __________. The shofar was __________. The cornett was another type of horn. These old instruments __________. But they were similar to modern-day brass instruments.

Organizer Listen to the talk again. Then, fill in the blanks with the correct words.

Renaissance Musical Instruments

- Stringed instruments
  - Included the lute, vihuela, rebec, and ⓐ __________
  - Modern guitar and ⓑ __________ evolved from them
- Woodwind instruments
  - Included the ⓒ __________ and transverse flute
  - ⓓ __________ evolved from it
- ⓔ __________ instruments
  - Included the sackbut, shofar, and cornett
  - Weren't made of metal but were ⓕ __________

Comprehension

Main Topic

Circle the correct answer.

1 What is the main topic of the talk?

ⓐ The people who played musical instruments during the Renaissance

ⓑ How Renaissance musical instruments evolved over time

ⓒ Some musical instruments popular during the Renaissance

Details

Answer the questions.

2 Which of the following was NOT a stringed instrument in the Renaissance?

ⓐ The rebec

ⓑ The cornett

ⓒ The vihuela

3 Which two musical instruments did the hurdy-gurdy resemble?

ⓐ The piano and guitar

ⓑ The violin and accordion

ⓒ The trombone and recorder

4 What was the shofar?

ⓐ It was a woodwind instrument.

ⓑ It was a brass instrument with a slide.

ⓒ It was a hollowed-out animal horn.

5 Fill in the blank with the correct word(s).

The modern-day __________________ evolved from the vihuela.

Vocabulary

Match the words and phrases with their definitions.

6 hollowed-out •	• ⓐ almost the same
7 remain •	• ⓑ a variety of
8 focus on •	• ⓒ having an empty space on the inside
9 similar •	• ⓓ to stay; to keep doing something
10 a wide range of •	• ⓔ to stress; to emphasize

Listening Skills Practice: Compare and Contrast I

What is compare and contrast?

Compare and contrast shows similarities and differences. A comparison shows a similarity between two people, places, or things. A contrast shows a difference between two people, places, or things. Look for words such as *than*, *more*, *both*, *neither*, and *too* to recognize comparisons or contrasts.

A **Write "compare" or "contrast" for the following sentences.**

ⓐ ______________ The viol was a Renaissance stringed instrument, and the rebec was, too.

ⓑ ______________ Both the flute and violin evolved from Renaissance musical instruments.

ⓒ ______________ The trumpet is made of metal, but the cornett was not.

B **Listen to another talk related to the topic and answer the questions.**

NOTE

1 Which of the following does the bagpipe NOT have?

ⓐ A melody pipe

ⓑ A large airtight bag

ⓒ A mallet

2 What does a hammered dulcimer look like?

ⓐ It is a board with strings stretched out over it.

ⓑ It is a brass instrument with a slide.

ⓒ It is a percussion instrument that a musician hits.

3 Match the sentences to make comparisons or contrasts.

ⓐ Both the bagpipe and hammered dulcimer	ⓘ a musician strikes the hammered dulcimer with two mallets.
ⓑ Many people hate the sound of the bagpipe	ⓘⓘ but enjoy the sound of the hammered dulcimer.
ⓒ While a musician blows air into a bagpipe,	ⓘⓘⓘ are Renaissance musical instruments.

Unit 20 Movie Soundtracks

Pre-Listening Questions

Answer the following questions.

1 What is a movie soundtrack?
2 What kind of music often appears in movies?
3 Why do movie directors put music in their films?
4 What are your favorite movie soundtracks? Why?

Vocabulary

Write the correct word or phrase from the box for each definition.

incredibly	run	suspense	purpose	talkie	sadden

1 ____________ very; highly
2 ____________ to make unhappy
3 ____________ a reason
4 ____________ to play a movie
5 ____________ a movie that has sound
6 ____________ a feeling of uncertainty or excitement

Movie Soundtracks

Listen to the talk. Fill in the blanks as you listen.

Almost all movies have music. The type of music varies. It may be ____________________, classical music, and even opera. It ____________________ of the movie. The music doesn't ____________________ though. Sometimes it plays while it doesn't at other times. Movie directors use music in their films ____________________. Music can ____________________ in a film. It can also be used to ____________________, and amuse viewers. All of the music in a film is called ____________________.

The first films ever made were ____________________. Because there was no sound, ____________________ while the films ran. In many cases, ____________________ performed for the viewers. When talkies—movies that had sound—came out ____________________, directors began including soundtracks in their films. Since then, the soundtrack has become ____________________. There are even awards given ____________________ for the best film music.

Most movie soundtracks ____________________. In addition, they sell just a few copies. ____________________ and sell millions of copies. The soundtrack to *The Sound of Music*, for instance, ____________________. So too have the soundtracks for the *Star Wars* movies.

Today, there are several individuals who ____________________. In general, the works they compose are ____________________. John Williams is probably ____________________ of film scores. Jerry Goldsmith, James Horner, and Ennio Morricone are three other famous film score composers.

Organizer **Listen to the talk again. Then, fill in the blanks with the correct words.**

Movie Soundtracks

- Include music such as pop songs, rock music, rap, classical music, and ⓐ ____________
- Doesn't play through ⓑ ____________ movie
- Can increase ⓒ ____________
- Can frighten, sadden, make happy, and ⓓ ____________ viewers

- Started to be included in films in the 1920s
- *The Sound of Music* and *Star Wars* soundtracks have sold ⓔ ____________ of copies
- Film score composers include ⓕ ____________, Jerry Goldsmith, James Horner, and Ennio Morricone

Circle the correct answer.

1 What is the main idea of the talk?

ⓐ The best film score composer is John Williams.

ⓑ Music can make films scarier or funnier.

ⓒ Soundtracks are an important part of films.

Details

Answer the questions.

2 Why do movie directors include music in their films?

ⓐ To increase the amount of suspense

ⓑ To make their films more popular

ⓒ To get more people to watch their movies

3 When did movie directors start using soundtracks?

ⓐ In the 1910s

ⓑ In the 1920s

ⓒ In the 1930s

4 Which person is NOT a film score composer?

ⓐ James Horner

ⓑ John Williams

ⓒ Steven Spielberg

5 Fill in the blank with the correct word(s).

The soundtracks to ____________________ and *Star Wars* have sold millions of copies.

Vocabulary

Match the words and phrases with their definitions.

6 silent movie •	• ⓐ to scare
7 frighten •	• ⓑ original music written for a movie
8 integral •	• ⓒ important
9 amuse •	• ⓓ a film that has no sound
10 film score •	• ⓔ to make a person laugh or have fun

Listening Skills Practice: Compare and Contrast II

What is compare and contrast?

Compare and contrast shows similarities and differences. Speakers often make comparisons and contrasts during their talks. Learn to recognize when speakers are doing this by listening for key words such as *and*, *but*, *however*, *both*, *neither*, and *also*.

A **Fill in the blanks with the correct word from the box.**

however	both	too

ⓐ ______________ John Williams and James Horner are popular film score composers.

ⓑ Most soundtracks sell few copies; ______________, some sell millions of copies.

ⓒ *The Sound of Music* soundtrack sold many copies, and *Star Wars* did, ______________.

B **Listen to a talk by a reporter related to the topic and answer the questions.**

NOTE

1 Which film score did John Williams NOT compose?

ⓐ *Raiders of the Lost Ark*

ⓑ *Star Trek*

ⓒ *E.T.*

2 Which statement about John Williams is correct?

ⓐ All of his soundtracks have sold more than one million copies.

ⓑ He helped Steven Spielberg direct some movies.

ⓒ He used to be the conductor for the Boston Pops.

3 Circle the correct word in each sentence.

ⓐ John Williams is a great conductor (so / yet) is more famous for his soundtracks.

ⓑ (Both / Neither) *Jaws* and *Star Wars* are two soundtracks that John Williams composed.

ⓒ John Williams composed the soundtracks for most of Steven Spielberg's movies (and / but) not all of them.

Answers

Answers

Chapter 1 Amazing Animals

Unit 01 Koko the Gorilla

p. 11

Pre-Listening Questions Sample Answer

1 It's a primate. Some other primates are monkeys, chimpanzees, and humans.

2 I have heard her name, but I don't know why she is famous.

3 I know some animals can use sign language to communicate with humans.

4 Yes, I would. I would love to talk to my dog and cat. I want to know what they are thinking.

Vocabulary

1	captivity	2	primate
3	tremendous	4	communicate
5	effort	6	handler

p. 12

Script

M Teacher: Humans have long wanted to communicate with animals. They've been able to do this to some extent. For instance, dogs can understand instructions such as "Sit," "Come," and "Roll over." Other tame animals can understand a small number of instructions. But animals can't speak to humans in any languages that people can understand.

Some scientists believed they could teach primates such as gorillas and chimpanzees to communicate with humans though. They did this by using American Sign Language. It's also called ASL. One of these gorillas was Koko. The effort to teach Koko to talk with humans has been a tremendous success.

Koko was born at the San Francisco Zoo in 1971. She has spent her entire life in captivity. Koko is a western lowland gorilla. In 1976, the Gorilla Foundation was established. Its mission was to teach two gorillas to communicate with humans by using ASL. Two gorillas were involved in the project: Koko and Michael. Both learned ASL, but Koko learned it much better than Michael.

In fact, Koko has learned more language than any other nonhuman has. She is still alive today although she is rather old for a gorilla. She knows more than 1,000 signs, and she can understand more than 2,000 words in English. Her handlers believe her IQ is between seventy and ninety-five. 100 is average for humans.

Koko is a unique animal. She has had a few pets—some cats and a bird—over the years. And she often displays emotions similar to those of humans. Researchers hope to teach her more in the future. And they hope to be able to speak with other animals as well.

Organizer

ⓐ 1971	ⓑ Michael
ⓒ 1,000	ⓓ 2,000
ⓔ 95	ⓕ a bird

p. 13

Comprehension

1	ⓒ	2	ⓐ	3	ⓒ
4	ⓑ	5	Gorilla Foundation		
6	ⓑ	7	ⓓ	8	ⓐ
9	ⓒ	10	ⓔ		

p. 14

Listening Skills Practice: Main Idea I

A ⓒ

B

Script

M Teacher: Gorillas aren't the only animals that have learned how to communicate with sign language. Chimpanzees have done it, too. In fact, the chimp Washoe was the first nonhuman ever to learn to use sign language. Washoe lived from 1965 to 2007. She spent most of her life in captivity. While she lived with various researchers, she learned to talk to them by using sign language. She learned around 350 words in American Sign Language. She also displayed behavior that was very humanlike at times. She enjoyed looking through catalogs. She particularly liked shoe catalogs. Washoe liked to brush her teeth, paint, and drink coffee as well. She also did something that impressed researchers very much. She taught another chimp how to use sign language. She taught the chimp Loulis his first sign only a few days after she met him. Researchers hope that they can get chimps to teach one another how to use sign language in the future.

1	ⓑ	2	ⓒ	3	ⓐ

Unit 02 Seeing-Eye Dogs

p. 15

Pre-Listening Questions Sample Answer

1 A blind man is using a seeing-eye dog to walk down the street.
2 They help blind people get around.
3 I think monkeys can help people do some activities.
4 I think service animals are great. They can help many people with disabilities have better lives.

Vocabulary

1	master	2	assist
3	breed	4	avoid
5	fortunate	6	bond

p. 16

Script

M Teacher: Many blind people have problems going from place to place. When they go outside, they use canes that they tap on the ground in front of them. This lets them avoid running into people or objects. Nevertheless, for these people, life can be quite difficult. Other blind people are more fortunate. They have seeing-eye dogs that assist them. Blind people with seeing-eye dogs can function well in society.

Seeing-eye dogs are trained to aid blind people. They can lead people down busy sidewalks and help them avoid hitting others. They can help people cross streets. Many of them can even press buttons on elevators. Basically, seeing-eye dogs act as the eyes of blind people and therefore improve their owners' daily lives.

Many breeds of dogs can become seeing-eye dogs. The first seeing-eye dogs were German shepherds. Golden retrievers and Labrador retrievers are often seeing-eye dogs, too. The dogs must be somewhat big and intelligent. They need to be in good health as well. Then, the dogs must attend a school. There, dog trainers teach them how to assist their future masters. Finally, the dog and its owner are matched. They train together for up to a month. That way, they can get used to each other.

Seeing-eye dogs and their owners frequently form close bonds. The dogs not only lead their owners around but also help relieve their owners' feelings of stress and loneliness. In addition, guide dogs are becoming more accepted around the world. So their owners can take them into lots of business establishments, including restaurants. Thus seeing-eye dogs greatly improve the quality of life of their owners.

Organizer

ⓐ trained	ⓑ cross streets
ⓒ loneliness	ⓓ eyes
ⓔ intelligent	ⓕ masters

p. 17

Comprehension

1	ⓒ	2	ⓑ	3	ⓐ
4	ⓐ	5	stress		
6	ⓔ	7	ⓑ	8	ⓐ
9	ⓒ	10	ⓓ		

p. 18

Listening Skills Practice: Main Idea II

A ⓒ

B

Script

M Student: For my report, I'm going to talk about service animals. Most people know about seeing-eye dogs. They assist blind people and help them get around. But there are other types of service animals as well. Two of the more common service animals are miniature horses and monkeys. Miniature horses are much smaller than regular horses. They can live indoors with people. Some people with disabilities use them as service animals. Miniature horses can lead blind people and can even pull wheelchairs. People who are allergic to dog hair often use them as service animals. In addition, capuchin monkeys are used as service animals these days. These monkeys are very good with their hands. So they are excellent for quadriplegics. Those are people who can't move their arms or legs. These service monkeys can do a variety of activities. They can put CDs into CD players, turn the pages of books, and even answer phones. Thanks to them, their owners can have much better lives.

1 ⓒ 2 ⓑ 3 ⓑ

Unit 03 Military Dolphins

p. 19

Pre-Listening Questions Sample Answer

1 It looks like the dolphin is obeying the soldier's command. Maybe the soldier is training it.
2 I'm not sure. Maybe they can swim with divers and help them.
3 I know the military uses dogs. I don't know about any other animals.
4 I think it's okay. But I hope that they treat the animals well.

Vocabulary

1	protect	2	researcher
3	mine	4	hull
5	detect	6	positive

p. 20

Script

W Teacher: One night, a terrorist puts on some scuba gear. He dives underwater and swims toward a navy base. His objective is an aircraft carrier. He wants to attach a bomb to the ship's hull. Then, it will explode and damage the ship. Suddenly, a dolphin swims by the terrorist. Then, a second dolphin appears. One dolphin stays near the terrorist while the other swims away. A moment later, several navy divers appear. They capture the terrorist and prevent the bomb from going off. But the real heroes are the dolphins. They found the terrorist.

This might sound like something from a science-fiction movie, but it isn't. Military dolphins are real. The United States Navy has been training dolphins since the 1960s. At first, the U.S. Navy studied dolphins and other sea animals to learn how they moved underwater. They wanted to make their ships and submarines move faster. Then, the researchers realized that they could train the dolphins to do various activities. So the U.S. Navy captured some dolphins and began training them.

The program has been successful. Dolphins are highly intelligent. They're among the most intelligent creatures on the planet. I also think they're amazing animals. I love the way that they swim and interact with humans. Anyway, the dolphins learned many skills. The U.S. Navy trained them to detect enemy divers as well as mines. Mines are bombs that can destroy large ships. The dolphins also learned to retrieve lost objects, to bring items to divers, and to protect ships and submarines. They helped the U.S. Navy in the Vietnam War as well as the first and second Gulf wars. I'm positive dolphins will be useful in the future as well.

Organizer

ⓐ U.S. Navy
ⓑ Captured
ⓒ mines
ⓓ lost objects
ⓔ submarines
ⓕ Gulf wars

p. 21

Comprehension

1 ⓑ 2 ⓐ 3 ⓒ
4 ⓐ 5 intelligent

6 ⓓ 7 ⓒ 8 ⓐ
9 ⓔ 10 ⓑ

p. 22

Listening Skills Practice: Fact and Opinion I

A ⓐ F ⓑ O ⓒ O

B

Script

M Teacher: Sea lions are mammals that live both on land and in the water. One common species is the California sea lion. It has four flippers and short hair, and it can weigh more than 300 kilograms. The California sea lion is a playful animal and often appears in animal shows at zoos and aquariums. Personally, I love watching them perform. But sea lions can do other valuable activities. For example, the U.S. Navy uses sea lions to protect its ships from enemy divers. They are an important part of the program called the Shallow Water Intruder Detection System. This is used to guard navy ships near shore. Sea lions are excellent swimmers. They are trained to swim behind an enemy diver. That way, the diver won't see them. Then, they put a clamp on the diver's arm or leg and swim away. A rope is attached to the clamp. Soldiers then pull on the rope and drag the diver out of the water. In that way, sea lions and humans work together to protect navy ships.

1 ⓒ
2 ⓑ
3 ⓐ ⓘⓘ ⓑ ⓘ ⓒ ⓘⓘⓘ

Unit 04

Bloodhounds

p. 23

Pre-Listening Questions Sample Answer

1 It looks like it is sniffing the ground. It might be chasing something.

2 I believe that they have very good noses.

3 I know shi-tzus, poodles, boxers, retrievers, and huskies. There are many types of dogs.

4 They can be good friends with humans. They can also work with the police. And some dogs work on farms, too.

Vocabulary

1 scent 2 evidence

3 relentless 4 convict

5 murderer 6 alley

p. 24

Script

W Teacher: Last night, a murderer escaped from the city jail. Many of the residents of the city were worried. They were afraid the police wouldn't catch him. I believed the police would be successful though. The reason is that they used a bloodhound to find him. It only took the bloodhound two hours to track down the missing prisoner. He was hiding in an alley a few kilometers away from the jail. The police recaptured him and took him back to prison. I'm sure it would have taken them longer if they didn't have a bloodhound on the police force.

Bloodhounds are my favorite breed of dog. They're very powerful and can weigh up to fifty kilograms. They have excellent personalities, and they make great pets, too. But the best part about them is their noses. They have incredibly sensitive noses. They often pick up strange scents and try to follow them. So they're a very curious breed. As a matter of fact, their curiosity can cause problems. Sometimes they smell something new and wander off in search of the source of the scent.

Bloodhounds frequently use their excellent noses to help humans. Many police forces use bloodhounds. Bloodhounds can pick up human scents that are 100 hours old. When they start tracking a scent, they are relentless. They never give up. Some bloodhounds have tracked down humans after traveling more than 160 kilometers. Courts all around the world accept evidence bloodhounds have found. In fact, one bloodhound was so effective that it helped convict more than 600 criminals.

Organizer

ⓐ 50 ⓑ sensitive

ⓒ wander off ⓓ police forces

ⓔ tracking ⓕ criminals

p. 25

Comprehension

1 ⓐ 2 ⓑ 3 ⓐ

4 ⓑ 5 scent

6 ⓒ 7 ⓐ 8 ⓓ

9 ⓑ 10 ⓔ

p. 26

Listening Skills Practice: Fact and Opinion II

A ⓐ O ⓑ F ⓒ F

B

Script

M Newscaster: Authorities have just announced they stopped a terrorist plot to destroy an airplane. This morning, a passenger on a plane going to London checked a bag onto the flight. The suitcase had a large bomb in it. According to a policeman, the bomb was big enough to destroy the plane. Unfortunately, human security guards didn't detect the bomb. Fortunately, the airport has a number of bomb-detection dogs. One of the dogs—named Friday—was on duty this morning. Friday sniffed something strange in the bag. So he alerted his handlers. Members of the bomb squad arrived. Then, they took the bomb apart. In addition, police arrested the man who tried to put the bomb onto the plane. Other airports around the country are making sure their bomb-detecting dogs are working hard in case there are other bombs like this one. It appears that Friday the dog has saved hundreds of people's lives. We'll have more on this breaking news story in just a few minutes.

1 ⓑ

2 ⓑ

3 ⓐ ⓘ ⓑ ⓘⓘⓘ ⓒ ⓘⓘ

Chapter 2 Famous Journeys

Unit 05 Ferdinand Magellan

p. 29

Pre-Listening Questions Sample Answer

1 He lived a long time ago. He was a sailor. He sailed around the world.
2 I think it would be very difficult. That ship looks small, and there were probably many men on it.
3 I have been on a ferry before. I enjoyed it, but the sea was calm.
4 I would like to take a journey in the jungle. I think it would be dangerous but exciting.

Vocabulary

1 mutiny 2 passageway
3 native 4 funds
5 reject 6 execute

p. 30

Script

M Teacher: After Christopher Columbus discovered the New World in 1492, many Europeans began to cross the Atlantic Ocean. One of these men was Ferdinand Magellan. Magellan was born in Portugal in 1480. As a young man, he sailed to India. But he did that by traveling south around Africa. Magellan believed he could get to India faster by sailing west across the Atlantic. He asked the king of Portugal for funds. But the king rejected Magellan. Magellan then asked King Charles V of Spain for assistance. Charles agreed, so Magellan prepared five ships.

In September 1519, more than 270 men set sail from Spain. First, they sailed to the Canary Islands. They're in the middle of the Atlantic Ocean. Then, they went south to South America. The ships sailed far to the south where it was very cold. The ships were running out of food. So some of the crew mutinied. But Magellan defeated them and executed the leaders of the mutiny.

Finally, Magellan found a passageway around the tip of South America. This place is called the Strait of Magellan. The water in this ocean was peaceful. Magellan decided to call it the Pacific Ocean. After four months of sailing, three of Magellan's ships arrived at the Mariana Islands. Then, the ships went to the Philippines. Magellan's crew got in a fight with the natives there though. Around forty men—and Magellan himself—were killed in the fight.

The survivors sailed west to return to Spain. They finished their journey in September 1522. Only one ship and eighteen sailors survived the trip. They became the first men ever to sail around the world.

Organizer

ⓐ Africa ⓑ west
ⓒ Portugal ⓓ the Pacific Ocean
ⓔ the Philippines ⓕ 18

p. 31

Comprehension

1 ⓒ 2 ⓐ 3 ⓒ
4 ⓑ 5 1519

6 ⓑ 7 ⓓ 8 ⓔ
9 ⓐ 10 ⓒ

p. 32

Listening Skills Practice: Sequencing I

A ⓐ 1 ⓑ 3 ⓒ 2

B

Script

W Teacher: The Strait of Magellan was one way to get to the Pacific Ocean. But sailing through it was dangerous. The weather was cold, and the water was rough, so many ships sank. As a result, the Europeans looked for other ways to get to the Pacific Ocean. Giovanni da Verrazano was one of these men who tried to find another way past the Americas. Although he was an Italian, he sailed to North America for the French. In 1524, he left France and sailed across the Atlantic. His goal was to explore the coast of North America from Florida in the south to Newfoundland in the north. He sailed around South Carolina and started drawing maps of the coast. Then, he headed north. He sailed into New York Bay and met some Native Americans there. After that, he sailed up to Newfoundland. Finally, he returned to France. He never found a way to the Pacific Ocean. But he succeeded in exploring a large part of the coast of North America.

1 ⓑ
2 ⓐ
3 ⓐ 2 ⓑ 1 ⓒ 3

Unit 06 Roald Amundsen

p. 33

Pre-Listening Questions Sample Answer

1 I'm not sure. I guess he was a traveler in a cold place.
2 I can see two men standing by a flag. They are in a very snowy area.
3 I don't know. I think it is too cold for me.
4 I think that Antarctica would be very cold. It might be beautiful, but it's still too cold for me.

Vocabulary

1 trek	2 tragic
3 desire	4 expedition
5 adventurous	6 airship

p. 34

Script

W Teacher: Some men prefer to remain home and rarely leave their hometowns. Others are more adventurous. Roald Amundsen was the latter. Born in Norway in 1872, Amundsen loved exploring the polar regions of the world.

Amundsen's first great adventure began in 1903. He was searching for the Northwest Passage. Ever since the Europeans discovered the Americas, they had sought the Northwest Passage. This was a way to get from the Atlantic Ocean to the Pacific Ocean by sailing north. Many men tried to find it. Yet none succeeded. Amundsen, however, found it during a journey that lasted three years.

Later, in 1910, Amundsen set his sights on the South Pole and sailed to Antarctica. On January 14, 1911, his ship arrived in Antarctica. His team began preparing for the trip. Then, on October 14, 1911, five men, fifty-two dogs, and four sleds began the trek to the bottom of the Earth. It was a difficult journey, but, on December 14, 1911, they made it. They were thirty-five days faster than a British expedition led by Robert Scott. All of Amundsen's men survived the return trip to their ship. Sadly, only eleven of the dogs survived.

Amundsen had a desire to reach the North Pole as well. In 1926, he teamed up with an Italian and an American. They used an airship to fly over the North Pole. As they flew above it, all three men dropped the flags of their countries onto the North Pole. Two years later, Amundsen's life came to a tragic end. He was on a rescue mission when his plane disappeared. Only pieces of the plane were found. Amundsen's body was never recovered.

Organizer

ⓐ January 14	ⓑ Five
ⓒ British	ⓓ December 14
ⓔ Italian	ⓕ the North Pole

p. 35

Comprehension

1 ⓑ	2 ⓑ	3 ⓐ
4 ⓒ	5 rescue	
6 ⓒ	7 ⓓ	8 ⓐ
9 ⓔ	10 ⓑ	

p. 36

Listening Skills Practice: Sequencing II

A ⓐ 2 ⓑ 3 ⓒ 1

B

Script

W Student: In the early 1900s, there was a race to the North Pole. Several adventurers wanted to be the first to get there. In 1908, Frederick Cook claimed that he and some others had made it to the North Pole. A year later in 1909, Robert Peary stated that his expedition had reached the North Pole, too. But most people believe neither man had actually gotten to the North Pole. Cook couldn't produce any evidence he had been there. As for Peary, he had poor navigational skills, and he likely never reached the North Pole even though he believed he had. In 1926, Richard Byrd announced that he had flown over the North Pole in an airplane. The journey was expected to take eighteen hours. Byrd, however, returned in fewer than sixteen hours. So many people think he never made it either. The first confirmed visit to the North Pole was therefore made by Roald Amundsen in 1926. He and two others did that a few days after Byrd's trip.

1 ⓒ
2 ⓐ
3 ⓐ 1 ⓑ 3 ⓒ 2

Unit 07 Captain Cook

p. 37

Pre-Listening Questions Sample Answer

1 He was a sailor. He captained a ship for England.
2 He lived a few centuries ago. I'm not exactly sure when.
3 Christopher Columbus is very famous. So are Magellan and Sir Francis Drake.
4 I think that would be fun. I would like to take a cruise to a tropical island.

Vocabulary

1 head
2 confirm
3 superior
4 apprentice
5 rumor
6 enlist

p. 38

Script

M Teacher: James Cook was born in England in 1728. While he grew up on a farm, Cook had no interest in agriculture. Instead, he was fascinated by the sea. After he turned eighteen, he went to sea as an apprentice on a merchant ship. Then, when the French and Indian War began, he enlisted in the Royal Navy.

Cook loved maps and was good at drawing them. While he was in the Royal Navy, his superiors noticed his mapmaking skills. Those skills enabled him to be given command of a ship. In 1768, he departed for the South Pacific Ocean on his first great expedition. During his trip, he visited Tahiti. He mapped most of the two main islands of New Zealand. And he visited the eastern coast of Australia. When he returned home, three years had passed.

In 1772, Cook set sail on his second expedition. It lasted until 1775. Cook had heard rumors of a continent south of Australia. He took the two ships on his expedition further south than anyone had sailed before. However, the weather was cold, and there was ice in the water, so the ships turned back and sailed home. Cook was unable to confirm the existence of land south of Australia.

In 1776, Cook went on his third and final expedition. He was searching for the Northwest Passage. He sailed up to Alaska but could not find a way into the Atlantic Ocean. Then, Cook and his crew headed south, where they landed in Hawaii in 1779. Unfortunately, Cook's men and the islanders got into a fight. One of the Hawaiians killed Cook and ended the life of one of England's greatest adventurers.

Organizer

ⓐ three
ⓑ New Zealand
ⓒ Australia
ⓓ cold weather
ⓔ 1776
ⓕ Hawaii

p. 39

Comprehension

1 ⓐ
2 ⓒ
3 ⓒ
4 ⓐ
5 Royal Navy
6 ⓑ
7 ⓓ
8 ⓐ
9 ⓔ
10 ⓒ

p. 40

Listening Skills Practice: Word Stress I

A
ⓐ Cook [loved] maps and was good at drawing them.
ⓑ When he returned home, three [years] had passed.
ⓒ He sailed up to Alaska but could [not] find a way into the Atlantic Ocean.

B

Script

M Teacher: The greatest river in North America is the Mississippi River. It flows south from the state of Minnesota down to Louisiana. There, it empties into the Gulf of Mexico. The Spanish discovered it in the 1500s. But they didn't sail very far upriver. Later, in 1673, two Frenchmen started to sail down the river. Their names were Jacques Marquette and Louis Joliet. They began their journey in what's now the American state of Wisconsin. Using canoes, they paddled down the Mississippi River. While they were traveling, they mapped much of the area. They had some encounters with Native Americans in the area. As they traveled south, the natives told them that some Spaniards were in the south. At that point, the two men realized that the river flowed into the Gulf of Mexico. Many people had believed that it flowed to the Pacific Ocean. Not wanting to fight the Spanish, they turned around and returned to the north.

1 ⓒ
2 ⓑ

3 ⓐ The greatest river in North America is the Mississippi River.
ⓑ At that point, the two men then realized that the river flowed into the Gulf of Mexico.
ⓒ Not wanting to fight the Spanish, they turned around and returned to the north.

Unit 08 Stanley and Livingstone

p. 41

Pre-Listening Questions Sample Answer

1 It looks like two men are greeting each other. Everyone else is watching them.
2 I believe that they were travelers in Africa.
3 People called Africa "the Dark Continent" because it was very mysterious and few people ever traveled there.
4 I would like to visit Egypt to see the pyramids and the Nile River. And I want to visit South Africa to see all of the different animals.

Vocabulary

1 porter 2 missionary
3 dense 4 inhospitable
5 presume 6 disaster

p. 42

Script

M Teacher: For centuries, people called Africa "the Dark Continent." Even though it was near Europe, the Europeans rarely traveled far from the coast. Much of the northern part of Africa is inhospitable desert. And the middle part is dense jungle filled with dangerous animals. It wasn't until the 1800s that the Europeans began to explore the interior of the continent.

Dr. David Livingstone was a Scottish missionary. He first went to Africa in 1841. He spent many years there and went on several trips around the continent. During his time there, he traveled through much of the interior. He discovered Victoria Falls. And he was one of the first people to make a transcontinental journey in Africa. Then, in 1866, Dr. Livingstone went on a journey to find the source of the Nile River. Unfortunately, it was a disaster. His porters deserted him. His supplies and medicines were stolen. And Livingstone became very sick.

Back in Europe, no one heard from Dr. Livingstone for a few years. People feared he was dead. So the *New York Herald*, an American newspaper, sent Henry Morgan Stanley to Africa. His goal was to find proof of Dr. Livingston's death. In 1871, Stanley started in Zanzibar. He had more than 200 porters and a great deal of equipment. Stanley's journey was almost as bad as Livingstone's. His porters deserted him. Others died of various diseases on a journey that covered more than 1,000 kilometers.

Finally, on November 10, 1871, Stanley entered Ujiji, a village in Tanzania. He saw a white man surrounded by Africans and Arabs. He then uttered the famous words, "Dr. Livingstone, I presume?" The man simply answered, "Yes."

Organizer

ⓐ Victoria Falls ⓑ source
ⓒ Disappeared ⓓ Dr. Livingston
ⓔ difficult ⓕ Ujiji

p. 43

Comprehension

1 ⓑ 2 ⓓ 3 ⓑ
4 ⓐ 5 newspaper
6 ⓔ 7 ⓒ 8 ⓑ
9 ⓐ 10 ⓓ

p. 44

Listening Skills Practice: Word Stress II

A ⓐ And Livingstone became very sick.
ⓑ Back in Europe, no one heard from Dr. Livingstone for a few years.
ⓒ Stanley's journey was almost as bad as Livingstone's.

B

Script

M Newscaster: Today, December 10, 2010, one of the great travelers of African rivers was lost when a crocodile attacked his boat and killed him. The man's name was Hendri Coetzee. He came from South Africa. At the time of his death, Coetzee was exploring the Lukuga River. It's in the Democratic Republic of Congo. Coetzee sailed up and down many of Africa's great rivers. An adventuresome person, he also enjoyed going over waterfalls in boats. But

Coetzee was most famous for a journey he made in 2004. On January 17 of that year, he led an expedition that started at Lake Victoria in Tanzania. He and his crew then sailed down the Nile River. Their journey lasted four and a half months. On May 21, they reached the Mediterranean Sea. They were the first people ever to sail the entire length of the Nile River from its beginning to its end.

1 ⓒ

2 ⓑ

3 ⓐ Today, December 10, 2010, one of the great travelers of African rivers was lost.

ⓑ An adventuresome person, he also enjoyed going over waterfalls in boats.

ⓒ They were the first people ever to sail the entire length of the Nile River from its beginning to its end.

Chapter 3 American Folklore

Unit 09 Pocahontas

p. 47

Pre-Listening Questions Sample Answer

1 It looks like some Indians are with some white colonists.

2 She was an American Indian. I don't know much about her though.

3 I know Squanto. And I know Sequoyah.

4 I would feel very angry. My country belongs to my people. People from another country should not try to colonize us.

Vocabulary

1 establish
2 celebrity
3 club
4 convert
5 clash
6 permanent

p. 48

Script

W Teacher: In 1607, the English established their first permanent colony in North America. The site was Jamestown, Virginia. There were more than 200 colonists, and their leader was Captain John Smith.

The colonists landed in a place with many Indian tribes. Many were unfriendly toward the colonists. They had met other Englishmen before, and those men had treated the Indians badly. So the Indians were hostile to the new colonists. As a result, the two sides often clashed with one another.

On one occasion, the members of a tribe captured John Smith. They took him to Powhatan. He was the tribe's leader. Powhatan decided to execute the captain. Some members of the tribe put Smith's head on a block. They prepared to beat him to death with clubs. Then, Pocahontas, one of Powhatan's daughters, went to Smith and put her head on top of his. In that way, she saved his life.

Pocahontas became friends with the colonists. In 1609, most of the colonists died during the harsh winter. But Pocahontas helped the colonists by giving them food. She warned them when some Indians were going to attack, too. Thanks to her, the colonists were prepared, so the attack never happened.

In 1612, the colonists captured Pocahontas while fighting with the Indians. During her time in captivity, she converted to Christianity. She also fell in love with John Rolfe, one of the colonists. The two got married and went to England in 1616. There, Pocahontas was a celebrity. While in England, she became sick though. She and her husband had planned to return to Virginia, but Pocahontas died in 1617 and never returned to her homeland.

Organizer

ⓐ leader
ⓑ Powhatan
ⓒ saved
ⓓ colonists
ⓔ got sick
ⓕ Christianity

p. 49

Comprehension

1 ⓑ
2 ⓑ
3 ⓒ
4 ⓐ
5 married

6 ⓑ
7 ⓓ
8 ⓐ
9 ⓒ
10 ⓔ

p. 50

Listening Skills Practice: Dictation I

A ⓐ the members of a tribe captured John Smith

ⓑ most of the colonists died during the harsh winter

ⓒ went to England in 1616

B

Script

M Teacher: In 1804, Meriweather Lewis and William Clark led an expedition to the western part of America. Their goal was to explore the land in the Louisiana Territory. The United States had just bought it from France. It was a difficult journey for all of the men on the trip. Fortunately, a woman named Sacajawea gave them a lot of help. She was a member of the Shoshone tribe. When she was young, another tribe kidnapped her. Then, they sold her to a French trapper. His name was Toussaint Charbonneau. The two later married, and Sacajawea gave birth to her son Jean-Baptiste. Lewis and Clark hired Charbonneau as a guide. They wanted Sacajawea to go, too. She spoke the Shoshone language. That made her a valuable translator. She helped to negotiate trades for supplies between the explorers and Indians. She also helped the expedition have peaceful relationships with the Indian tribes they met on their journey. Thanks in part to Sacajawea, the Lewis and Clark Expedition was a big success.

1 ⓒ

2 ⓐ

3 ⓐ explore the land in the Louisiana Territory
ⓑ gave them a lot of help
ⓒ supplies between the explorers and Indians

Unit 10 Johnny Appleseed

p. 51

Pre-Listening Questions Sample Answer

1 A person is planting a tree in the ground.

2 From his name, I guess that he planted many apple trees.

3 I think it would be nice for a while, but then it would become boring. I like to be around lots of my friends.

4 No, I wouldn't. I would get lonely. I prefer life in the city with many people.

Vocabulary

1	inland	2	orchard
3	frontier	4	folklore
5	serve	6	settler

p. 52

Script

M Teacher: The American Midwest includes the states of Ohio, Indiana, and Illinois. Many people don't think of them as being in the west. However, in the 1700s and part of the 1800s, they were the frontier in America. The reason is that the early American colonies were all by the Atlantic Ocean. So few people ever went far inland.

The people who did travel in the interior part of America were often very colorful characters. They tended to be adventurous. And they often had interesting stories. Johnny Appleseed was one of these people.

His real name was John Chapman. He was born in Massachusetts in 1774. When he was young, he served as an apprentice in an orchard. There, he learned about apples. At the age of eighteen, he left Massachusetts and headed west. First, he lived in western Pennsylvania. He began planting apple trees. He didn't simply plant trees anywhere though. Instead, he planted groups of apple trees and took care of them for a year or two. Then, as settlers arrived in the area, he sold the trees to them.

Thanks to his love of apple trees, people called him Johnny Appleseed. Johnny soon left Pennsylvania and went west to Ohio. He traveled all around Ohio and planted numerous apple trees. Johnny had a great love of nature. He lived simply, too. He wore cloth sacks for clothes and a cooking pot for a hat. The Indians who saw him respected his love of nature. Even when they were fighting settlers, they left Johnny alone. Today, Johnny Appleseed is one of the most famous figures from American folklore.

Organizer

ⓐ orchard	ⓑ Pennsylvania
ⓒ settlers	ⓓ Ohio
ⓔ Indians	ⓕ famous figure

p. 53

Comprehension

1	ⓐ	2	ⓒ	3	ⓑ
4	ⓐ	5	cooking pot		
6	ⓓ	7	ⓑ	8	ⓔ
9	ⓒ	10	ⓐ		

p. 54

Listening Skills Practice: Dictation II

A ⓐ they were the frontier in America

ⓑ he served as an apprentice in an orchard

ⓒ respected his love of nature

B

Script

M Student: Paul Bunyan is my favorite person from American folklore. In the late 1800s and early 1900s, large parts of the United States were covered with forests. People often cut down the trees and used the wood to make homes, furniture, and other products. Lumberjacks were the people who cut the trees down. Paul Bunyan was a mythical lumberjack. People told lots of stories about him starting around 1910. Paul Bunyan was an enormous and powerful man. Even as a baby, he liked chopping trees down. He had a giant blue ox named Babe. The two of them were always together. This is one of my favorite stories about Paul Bunyan. According to legends, he created the Grand Canyon. How did he do that? Simple. He and Babe were walking one day, and Paul let his ax drag on the ground behind him. He also created the Great Lakes. Why did he do that? He needed a place for Babe to be able to drink water from.

1 ⓐ

2 ⓒ

3 ⓐ favorite person from American folklore

ⓑ he liked chopping trees down

ⓒ let his ax drag on the ground behind him

Unit 11 The First Thanksgiving

p. 55

Pre-Listening Questions Sample Answer

1 It looks like they are having a feast. One woman is giving the Indians some food.

2 It is a big holiday in America. It is in November. And Americans usually eat lots of food, including turkey, on Thanksgiving.

3 Yes, there is. In Korea, we celebrate *Chuseok*. It is a three-day-long holiday in the fall. We celebrate it because of the fall harvest.

4 We often go to our hometowns and meet our relatives. Many families have special ceremonies for their ancestors. And people eat lots of good food during *Chuseok*.

Vocabulary

1	harmful	2	harvest
3	store	4	sap
5	beneficial	6	feast

p. 56

Script

W Teacher: In 1620, a group of people called the Pilgrims got on the ship the *Mayflower*. There were 110 Pilgrims. They set sail on September 6 and arrived in America on November 10. They landed in Plymouth in what later became the Massachusetts Bay Colony.

Their first winter in Massachusetts was dreadful. Fewer than fifty Pilgrims survived the cold, snowy winter weather. The next year in March, an Indian walked into their camp. He looked at them and said, "Welcome." The Pilgrims were surprised he knew English. His name was Samoset. He and another Indian, Squanto, assisted the Pilgrims. They showed the Pilgrims how to plant Indian corn and other crops. They taught the Pilgrims how to get sap from maple trees. And they showed the Pilgrims which wild plants were harmful and which ones were beneficial.

That fall, the Pilgrims had an excellent harvest. They had plenty of food to eat and enough food to store for the winter. They had a large amount of fish and meat. The Pilgrims had built a large number of homes and other buildings as well. They decided to celebrate by having a large feast. They prepared all kinds of food. They invited Samoset, Squanto, and many other Indians. Around ninety Indians showed up for the event. For three days, the Pilgrims and Indians celebrated. They ate food and played many games. That was the first Thanksgiving in America.

Today, Thanksgiving is a national holiday. Americans celebrate it on the fourth Thursday of November every year. It's one of the most important holidays in the country.

Organizer

ⓐ Plymouth	ⓑ died
ⓒ Samoset	ⓓ harvest
ⓔ Ate	ⓕ three days

p. 57

Comprehension

1 ⓒ 2 ⓒ 3 ⓑ
4 ⓒ 5 *Mayflower*

6 ⓑ 7 ⓐ 8 ⓔ
9 ⓒ 10 ⓓ

p. 58

Listening Skills Practice: Guessing Unknown Words I

A ⓑ

B

Script

W Teacher: One of the most famous of all American Indians is Squanto. He was a member of the Patuxet tribe that lived in Massachusetts. In 1614, he left America with Thomas Hunt and went to Spain. He was probably a slave then. However, he escaped and traveled to England. In England, he learned to speak English. Later, in 1617, he traveled to Newfoundland and then returned to England. He finally went back to his tribe in 1619. Unfortunately, many of them had died from the disease smallpox. When the Pilgrims arrived, Massasoit, the leader of a nearby tribe, sent Squanto to meet them. Squanto surprised the Pilgrims because he spoke English so well. He also provided lots of assistance for them. Without Squanto, the Pilgrims might not have survived the first year. Sadly, Squanto became sick in 1622 and died soon afterward. The Pilgrims were saddened because of his death. Today, Americans still remember Squanto and the assistance he provided to the Pilgrims.

1 ⓒ 2 ⓑ 3 ⓒ

Unit 12 Davy Crockett

p. 59

Pre-Listening Questions Sample Answer

1 He looks like he enjoys the outdoors. He also looks like he enjoys a simple life.
2 I think he was probably a hunter because of his gun.
3 I know that it was difficult and dangerous. It was also probably very lonely.
4 There were changes in the class system in the late Joseon period. Some people in the lower level got rich from agriculture and commerce and bought their way up. In addition, government slaves called *gongnobi* were released.

Vocabulary

1 territory 2 scout
3 reputation 4 wild
5 represent 6 cattle

p. 60

Script

M Teacher: In the late 1700s and early 1800s, lots of Americans began moving west. They moved to territories such as Ohio, Indiana, Kentucky, and Tennessee. These lands were wild and dangerous. But many people didn't mind living on the frontier.

In 1786, Davy Crockett was born to a family that lived on the frontier in Tennessee. He grew up on a farm and was driving cattle to Virginia when he was only twelve. Crockett's father was hard on him though, so he ran away from home as a young boy. He lived in Virginia for a while and got married. But he soon moved back to Tennessee.

In Tennessee, he began to develop a reputation as a frontiersman. He served in the military to fight hostile Indians. As a soldier, he was a scout. He was also an outstanding hunter. People easily recognized him by the coonskin cap he wore on his head.

Crockett realized that the people living on the frontier needed a spokesperson. So he decided to represent them. He got involved in politics. First, he served in the Tennessee legislature. Later, he represented the state of Tennessee in the U.S. Congress. He served in the House of Representatives.

In 1836, he lost an election, so he left Washington, D.C. He and his family then moved to Texas. Texas had just declared its independence from Mexico. In response, Mexican soldiers invaded parts of Texas. Crockett went to the Alamo in San Antonio, Texas. The Mexican army surrounded it and attacked. Crockett died at the Alamo on March 6, 1836. After his death, people began telling a number of legends and stories about his accomplishments.

Organizer

ⓐ his father ⓑ Ran away
ⓒ Served ⓓ spokesperson
ⓔ the U.S. Congress ⓕ Texas

p. 61

Comprehension

1 ⓒ 2 ⓐ 3 ⓑ
4 ⓑ 5 Alamo

6 ⓒ 7 ⓔ 8 ⓐ
9 ⓓ 10 ⓑ

p. 62

Listening Skills Practice: Guessing Unknown Words II

A ⓐ

B

Script

M Tour Guide: Welcome to the Alamo. The Alamo is one of the most famous places in Texas. It was built in the 1700s. It was originally a Spanish mission and school. But it didn't become famous until 1836. When Texas declared its independence, the Mexicans were displeased. So they sent an army into Texas. The army's leader, Santa Anna, took his forces to San Antonio. The Texans sought protection here in the Alamo. From February 23 to March 6, the Mexicans besieged the Alamo. There were roughly 200 men defending the Alamo. But there were 6,000 Mexican soldiers. On March 6, the Mexican army broke though the walls and got into the Alamo. All of the defenders died. Some of them were great Texans such as Jim Bowie and Colonel William Travis. Davy Crockett died here as well. The Mexicans won the battle, but the Texans had a new battle cry. "Remember the Alamo," they said. Led by General Sam Houston, the Texans quickly defeated the Mexicans and remained independent.

1 ⓒ 2 ⓑ 3 ⓐ

Chapter 4 Historical Mysteries

Unit 13 The Lost Colony of Roanoke

p. 65

Pre-Listening Questions Sample Answer

1 I see some destroyed buildings. I guess no one lives in them now.
2 I guess the people could disappear and not leave a message for people who might come later.
3 I think it would be difficult. You would probably be very far away from your home.
4 Yes, I would. I think it would be exciting to live in another country.

Vocabulary

1 carve 2 colonize
3 plant 4 nobody
5 governor 6 establish

p. 66

Script

W Teacher: In 1607, some men and women successfully established the first permanent English colony in North America. The name of the colony was Jamestown. Jamestown wasn't the first English attempt to colonize an area in North America though. Twenty years earlier, some people tried to found a colony south of Jamestown. The name of the place was Roanoke Island.

Roanoke Island is located off the coast of the American state of North Carolina. In 1585, a group of Englishmen attempted to start a colony there. Sadly, they didn't get along well with the natives. And founding the colony was too hard for them. So they left a group of soldiers behind and sailed back to England. Strangely, the soldiers quickly disappeared, and nobody ever saw them again.

Two years later, in 1587, a new group of settlers arrived. They saw the burned ruins of the first colony on Roanoke Island. That sight upset them. Unfortunately, they arrived too late in the year to plant any crops. Yet there was some good news. On August 15, 1587, Virginia Dare was born. She was the first English child born in North America.

A few days later, John White, the governor of the colony, left. He returned to England to get more supplies. He wanted to return quickly. But he didn't go back to Roanoke for three years. When he arrived, everyone was gone. There weren't even any bodies. White searched carefully. All he found was one word carved into a tree: CROATAN. It was the name of a local Indian tribe. But the colonists weren't there. To this day, no one knows what happened to the lost colony of Roanoke.

Organizer

ⓐ North Carolina ⓑ 1585
ⓒ returned ⓓ 1587
ⓔ John White ⓕ CROATAN

p. 67

Comprehension

1 ⓑ 2 ⓐ 3 ⓒ
4 ⓒ 5 disappeared

6 ⓔ 7 ⓒ 8 ⓑ
9 ⓐ 10 ⓓ

p. 68

Listening Skills Practice: Paraphrasing I

A ⓒ

B

Script

M Teacher: In 53 B.C., a Roman army was defeated at the Battle of Carrhae in Turkey. Most of the Roman soldiers were killed. But 10,000 of them became prisoners. They were taken east and were never heard from again. Many historians have wondered what happened to the lost legion of Rome. Some believe the legion went to China. In the year 36 B.C., a Chinese army defeated a Hun army. A Chinese general wrote about a strange practice some of the soldiers they had captured had. They fought in rows and covered one another with their shields. That was a common Roman method of fighting. The Chinese took those soldiers and sent them east to Liqian. That might be the modern-day city of Zhelaizhai. Archaeologists digging there have unearthed Roman coins and pottery. They have also found bodies with Western features. The bodies are those of tall men with blond hair and blue eyes. It's highly likely that these archaeologists have finally found the lost legion.

1 ⓑ 2 ⓑ 3 ⓐ

Unit 14 Amelia Earhart

p. 69

Pre-Listening Questions Sample Answer

1 She was a pilot. She lived a long time ago. She disappeared somewhere while she was flying her airplane.

2 The airplane looks old. I don't think it would be very safe.

3 I guess that they crashed a lot. So they probably were not very safe.

4 Yes, I have been. Once, I was walking in the forest, and I got lost. I was very scared until I finally got out of the forest.

Vocabulary

1 relatively 2 navigator
3 flight 4 impressed
5 crash 6 accomplish

p. 70

Script

M Teacher: In 1908, an eleven-year-old girl named Amelia Earhart saw her first airplane. She wasn't impressed at all. More than a decade later in 1920, Amelia went to an airshow in California. There, she took her first flight. From then on, flying became her life.

At that time, airplanes were relatively new. Amelia worked hard, saved money, and bought her first plane. She quickly started setting records. She became the first female pilot to fly more than 14,000 feet above the ground. That's more than 4,200 meters high. In 1928, she became the first woman to fly across the Atlantic Ocean. She wasn't the only one on the plane, so it wasn't a solo flight. It wasn't until 1932 that she managed to fly solo across the Atlantic. She was the second person after Charles Lindbergh to accomplish that feat.

Earhart wasn't satisfied, so she decided to fly all the way around the world. She planned to do this with Fred Noonan, who was her navigator. She started in Miami, Florida, in June 1937. She made it across Africa and Asia. Then, she arrived in New Guinea. That's an island in the South Pacific. On July 2, Earhart and Noonan took off. Nobody ever saw them again.

There are many theories about what happened. Most people believe her plane crashed into the sea. Some say the Japanese captured Earhart and Noonan and then executed them for being American spies. Others think they landed on a desert island and lived there until they died. And a few individuals even claim that aliens in UFOs abducted them. One thing is certain: Nobody knows exactly what happened to the two of them.

Organizer

ⓐ first flight ⓑ records
ⓒ the Atlantic ⓓ New Guinea
ⓔ Nobody ⓕ Disappeared

p. 71

Comprehension

1 ⓒ	2 ⓒ	3 ⓑ
4 ⓑ	5 theories	
6 ⓔ	7 ⓒ	8 ⓐ
9 ⓑ	10 ⓓ	

p. 72

Listening Skills Practice: Paraphrasing II

A ⓑ

B

Script

M Newscaster: We interrupt this broadcast to bring you a breaking news story. French authorities have confirmed they have found the missing plane flown by Antoine de Saint-Exupery. Saint-Exupery is best known for his classic children's book *The Little Prince*. However, he was also a military pilot during World War II. On July 31, 1944, he was flying his plane, a Lockheed Lightning P-38. His plane, however, vanished without a trace. Decades later in 1998, a French fisherman found a bracelet with Saint-Exupery's name on it. He got it in the water near Marseilles, France. Then, a diver remembered having seen a crashed plane in the water back in the 1980s. Finally, there was an attempt to recover the plane. On this day, April 7, 2004, experts now know for sure that they have located Saint-Exupery's plane. The number on the body of the wrecked plane matches that of the plane Saint-Exupery was flying when he disappeared. His body wasn't recovered though. So what happened to it is still a mystery.

1 ⓐ	2 ⓑ	3 ⓐ

Unit 15 Atlantis

p. 73

Pre-Listening Questions Sample Answer

1 Atlantis was an island. It existed a long time ago.

2 Nobody knows. Many people say it was in the Atlantic Ocean though.

3 Something caused Atlantis to sink beneath the ocean.

4 I don't know. No one has ever found it. But I think it would be great if it really existed a long time ago.

Vocabulary

1 vast	2 civilization
3 philosopher	4 destruction
5 tsunami	6 simply

p. 74

Script

W Teacher: More than 10,000 years ago, there was an island civilization in the Atlantic Ocean. Each of its founders was half man and half god. The people of the island built ships and had a powerful navy. The island itself had a vast amount of gold, silver, and other precious metals. There were many exotic animals living there, too. In the center of the island was a great capital city. This was Atlantis. It was the greatest civilization in the ancient world. Then, one day, the people of Atlantis did something to upset the gods. So the gods caused the destruction of Atlantis. In a single night, the island sank beneath the water.

The Greek philosopher Plato told the story of Atlantis in two works more than 2,300 years ago. Since then, others have added to the story. But the most important question about Atlantis is this: Did it really exist? No one is sure of the answer.

Many people claim Atlantis actually existed. For instance, some believe it was located in the Mediterranean Sea. They say that it sank when a volcano on the island of Thera erupted around 1500 B.C. That eruption, people believe, caused a tsunami that sank Atlantis. Others think Atlantis was in the Atlantic Ocean. They believe it was near Spain or somewhere around Bimini Island off the coast of Florida, USA. But lots of people think Plato simply made up the story. They claim that Atlantis is a myth. They also point out that no one has ever found any evidence Atlantis existed.

Nevertheless, people continue to search for the lost land. Some of them truly believe they will find proof of the existence of Atlantis someday.

Organizer

ⓐ civilization	ⓑ upset
ⓒ two	ⓓ No one
ⓔ Mediterranean	ⓕ proof

p. 75

Comprehension

1 ⓐ 2 ⓑ 3 ⓑ
4 ⓒ 5 civilization

6 ⓒ 7 ⓔ 8 ⓐ
9 ⓑ 10 ⓓ

p. 76

Listening Skills Practice: Supporting Details I

A ⓐ too ⓑ For instance ⓒ also

B

Script

M Teacher: More than 100 kilometers northwest of Las Vegas, Nevada, is one of the most mysterious places in the United States. The official name is Groom Lake. But most people know it as Area 51. Few people have ever gained access to Area 51. And even fewer have ever spoken about it. In fact, the United States government only recently confirmed that the place exists. There are many theories about the purpose of Area 51. Some say the U.S. military tests new weapons and aircraft there. In addition, others believe scientists there do research concerning aliens and alien artifacts. Some people have claimed they worked on alien spacecraft while they were at Area 51. Others state they have actually seen aliens in Area 51. There are all kinds of rumors about the place. What's true? Nobody knows. It's impossible for civilians to get near the place. Anytime people get close to Area 51, armed guards appear and tell them to go away. Surely the government is hiding something mysterious there.

1 ⓒ
2 ⓑ
3 ⓐ ⓘⓘ ⓑ ⓘⓘⓘ ⓒ ⓘ

Unit 16 The Bermuda Triangle

p. 77

Pre-Listening Questions Sample Answer

1 It's a triangle that connects three places in the Atlantic Ocean. One of them is Bermuda. The other is Florida. I don't know the third one.

2 Yes, I have. My family and I visited Florida once. It was really beautiful there.

3 I guess they might have some kind of mechanical problems.

4 I don't know any mysterious places in my country. I think it would be fun to visit though.

Vocabulary

1 determine 2 fear
3 vanish 4 graveyard
5 instance 6 wreckage

p. 78

Script

W Teacher: Draw a line from the tip of southern Florida to Bermuda. Then, draw a line from Bermuda to Puerto Rico and one going back to Florida. That forms a triangle. It's known as the Bermuda Triangle or the Devil's Triangle. Many sailors and airmen fear going there. The reason is that, in around five centuries, more than 1,000 ships and planes have disappeared in the Bermuda Triangle.

Sometimes ships sink, and planes crash. But people can usually determine why the ships sank and why the planes crashed. In the Bermuda Triangle though, ships often suddenly sink in clear weather. Planes also vanish for no reason. In most cases, no wreckage is found either. It's like the ships and planes simply disappeared from the Earth itself.

For example, in 1918, the *U.S.S. Cyclops* was sailing with a crew of 309 people. Somewhere in the Bermuda Triangle, it vanished without a trace. Decades later, one of the most famous events involving the Bermuda Triangle occurred. On December 5, 1945, Flight 19 took off from a naval base in Florida. There were five Avenger bombers in the group. They were flying a training mission in clear weather. In the middle of the flight, radio contact with all five planes was lost. Nothing was ever heard from any of the men on the planes again. Nor were the planes found. That same night, two airplanes were sent out to rescue the missing planes. One of those planes disappeared.

There have been numerous strange instances like that. No one knows what makes the Bermuda Triangle a graveyard for ships and planes. That makes it one of the most mysterious places on the Earth.

Organizer

ⓐ Florida ⓑ feared
ⓒ 1,000 ⓓ 1918
ⓔ Flight 19 ⓕ rescue plane

p. 79

Comprehension

1 ⓑ 2 ⓐ 3 ⓑ
4 ⓒ 5 graveyard

6 ⓓ 7 ⓒ 8 ⓐ
9 ⓔ 10 ⓑ

p. 80

Listening Skills Practice: Supporting Details II

A ⓐ SD ⓑ SD ⓒ MI

B

Script

M Student: Some people believe in ghosts. But what about ghost ships? Do ghost ships exist? More than 100 years ago, people claimed that the *Mary Celeste* was a ghost ship. On November 7, 1872, the ship departed New York City. The ship's captain, wife, daughter, and seven crewmen were aboard. The ship was bound for Genoa, Italy. On December 4, 1872, the *Mary Celeste* was discovered by another ship. No one was aboard. Only the ship's papers and some equipment were missing. Its cargo was still onboard, and so were the crew members' possessions. Nobody knows what happened to the *Mary Celeste*. One theory is that pirates killed the crew. But why didn't they take the valuables and cargo? Another theory is that the crew feared for their lives, so they quickly abandoned ship. But what was the reason? There are even theories that aliens abducted them or sea monsters killed everyone. The truth is that no one knows what happened to the crew of the *Mary Celeste*.

1 ⓒ
2 ⓒ
3 ⓐ discovered ⓑ possessions ⓒ pirates

Chapter 5 Music

Unit 17 Louis Armstrong

p. 83

Pre-Listening Questions Sample Answer

1 I think he's playing the trumpet.
2 He was a jazz musician. He sang *What a Wonderful World*.
3 There are many genres of music. There are jazz, pop, rock, heavy metal, classical, and country music. There are many other genres, too.
4 I like pop and rock music. I like the way that they sound.

Vocabulary

1 hit 2 distinct
3 popularize 4 obvious
5 cornet 6 quartet

p. 84

Script

W Teacher: Louis Armstrong had one of the most distinct voices in all music. Today, most people only remember him for his song *What a Wonderful World*. He actually recorded that song in the last few years of his life. And it didn't even become a hit until more than a decade after Armstrong died. It's unfortunate that people don't know more about Armstrong than that one song.

Louis Armstrong was born in New Orleans, Louisiana, in 1901. New Orleans is often called "the birthplace of jazz." The musical tradition in New Orleans greatly affected Armstrong. When he was only eleven years old, he dropped out of school. He started playing music with a quartet of boys. They sang on the street and earned money from people passing by.

Armstrong soon learned to play the cornet. It's a musical instrument similar to the trumpet. He became an amazing cornet player. Armstrong soon began performing in places other than New Orleans. He played on steamboats going up and down the Mississippi River. He went to Chicago and New York City as well. His talent was obvious to everyone who saw him play.

One time in Chicago, Louis was recording a song. He suddenly dropped the lyric sheet. Instead of stopping, Louis continued singing. But he didn't sing the words. He just made up sounds. This was known as scat singing. Armstrong popularized that form of music. During his life, he became very famous. He recorded many hit songs, and he performed almost up until his death in 1971. Today, while he isn't as well-known as he once was, he's still remembered as one of the great musicians of the twentieth century.

Organizer

ⓐ New Orleans ⓑ quartet

ⓒ cornet ⓓ lyric sheet
ⓔ singing ⓕ scat

p. 85

Comprehension

1 ⓒ 2 ⓒ 3 ⓑ
4 ⓐ 5 birthplace

6 ⓑ 7 ⓓ 8 ⓒ
9 ⓔ 10 ⓐ

p. 86

Listening Skills Practice: Outlining I

A ⓐ tradition ⓑ quartet ⓒ cornet
ⓓ Performed ⓔ lyric sheet

B

Script

W Teacher: Like Louis Armstrong, Ella Fitzgerald was a jazz musician. She also had a voice that was easy to recognize. Born in 1917, she lived until 1996. During her singing career, she sold millions of albums and won numerous awards. She was called "the queen of jazz" and "the first lady of song" because of her incredible voice. At the age of sixteen, Fitzgerald made her singing debut in New York City. She performed at the famed Apollo Theater in Harlem. She mostly performed jazz music. But she was skilled in other genres as well. For instance, she performed bebop, soul, gospel, and the blues. She was an accomplished scat musician. She frequently awed people by the way she sang. Fitzgerald enjoyed singing solo, but she joined with many other famous musical artists of the day. She and Louis Armstrong made a number of hit songs. She also sang with Dizzy Gillespie and Billie Holiday, among others.

1 ⓐ jazz ⓑ millions ⓒ queen
ⓓ genres ⓔ gospel

Unit 18 George Frideric Handel

p. 87

Pre-Listening Questions Sample Answer

1 An orchestra is playing some music.
2 He was a classical music composer.
3 He composed *The Messiah*. He also lived in England in the 1700s.
4 I like some classical music. I don't know much about it. But some pieces of classical music sound very nice. I especially like some of Mozart's music.

Vocabulary

1 harpsichord 2 act
3 barge 4 patron
5 conduct 6 request

p. 88

Script

M Teacher: George Frideric Handel was born in Germany in 1685. His father wanted him to become a lawyer. Handel was more interested in music though. As a child, he took music lessons. He learned to play the harpsichord, violin, oboe, and organ. And he learned how to compose music. Despite his apparent musical skill, Handel began studying law. A year later, his father died, so Handel stopped his study of law and began focusing on music.

His true love was Italian opera, so he spent four years in Italy learning about it. Then, in 1710, Prince George of Hanover hired him to produce music. In 1714, Prince George would become King George I of England. By that time, Handel himself was living permanently in England. He had many English patrons, so he composed music, especially operas, for them.

It was in England that Handel wrote his greatest pieces of music. In 1717, he conducted Water Music for the first time. The orchestra played on a barge in the middle of the Thames River as King George I himself watched. The king loved the music so much that he requested to hear it several times.

Years later, in 1741, Handel finished work on *The Messiah*. It was an oratorio. An oratorio is a musical piece that often has a religious theme. An orchestra performs, and there are solo and choral works, but the singers don't act like they do in operas. Handel wrote more than twenty oratorios in his life. *The Messiah* ranks as the greatest and most popular of them all. On April 14, 1759, a few days after conducting a performance of *The Messiah*, Handel died.

Organizer

ⓐ Father ⓑ instruments
ⓒ died ⓓ English patrons
ⓔ oratorios ⓕ *The Messiah*

p. 89

Comprehension

1 ⓒ 2 ⓒ 3 ⓐ
4 ⓑ 5 lawyer

6 ⓒ 7 ⓔ 8 ⓐ
9 ⓓ 10 ⓑ

p. 90

Listening Skills Practice: Outlining II

A ⓐ lessons ⓑ England ⓒ operas
ⓓ requested ⓔ greatest

B

Script

M Usher: Thank you all for coming to tonight's performance of *The Messiah*. In just a moment, I'll open the doors. Then, you can go in to find your seats. But let me tell you a bit about it first. George Frideric Handel composed *The Messiah* in 1741. The oratorio tells the story of the life, death, and resurrection of Jesus Christ. Handel took all of the words in *The Messiah* from the King James Bible. He created a masterpiece. Today, it's one of the most performed works in all Western music. Amazingly, Handel only took twenty-four days to compose the music for *The Messiah*. The most recognizable piece from *The Messiah* is the *Hallelujah* chorus. According to stories, King George II of England attended a performance of *The Messiah* one time. He was so touched by the *Hallelujah* chorus that he stood up in the middle of it. Since the king stood, everyone else did the same. Since then, audiences around the world rise for the performing of the *Hallelujah* chorus.

1 ⓐ death ⓑ King James Bible ⓒ twenty-four
ⓓ touched ⓔ Stood

Unit 19 Renaissance Musical Instruments

p. 91

Pre-Listening Questions Sample Answer

1 I don't know the first instrument. The second instrument looks like an old guitar. And the third instrument looks like an old trombone.

2 The first two are stringed instruments. The last one is a brass instrument.

3 I know they played the harp during the Renaissance. They also played some kinds of flutes as well as the bagpipe.

4 I would like to play the first one. I don't know its name, but it looks really cool.

Vocabulary

1 bow 2 funeral
3 strum 4 resemble
5 emphasize 6 evolve

p. 92

Script

W Teacher: The Renaissance began around 1400 and lasted about 200 years. There were many advances in life in Europe during it. People focused on art, science, engineering, and math. They also emphasized music. During the Renaissance, people played a wide range of musical instruments. Some of these instruments later evolved into the modern ones that people play today.

Stringed musical instruments were very popular at that time. The lute was probably the most common of them. It resembled a modern-day guitar. In fact, the guitar evolved from the vihuela, a Spanish lute. A person played the lute by strumming the strings with his or her fingers. The viol and rebec were two other stringed instruments that people played then. To make music with them, the musicians moved a bow across the strings. The modern-day violin developed from the rebec. Finally, the hurdy-gurdy was a unique stringed instrument. It looked like a violin, but it also had keys like an accordion.

Woodwind instruments are among the oldest of all musical instruments. So it's no surprise that people played them during the Renaissance. The recorder, which remains popular today, was played by many musicians. People played the recorder at events such as festivals and funerals. The transverse flute, which later became the modern flute, was another woodwind from that time.

Brass instruments such as the trumpet and trombone didn't exist in the past. Instead, some people played the sackbut. Like the trombone, it had a slide that musicians could move back and forth. The shofar was a simple hollowed-out animal horn. The cornett was another type of horn. These old instruments weren't made of metal. But they were similar to modern-day brass instruments.

Organizer

ⓐ hurdy-gurdy ⓑ violin
ⓒ recorder ⓓ Modern flute
ⓔ Brass ⓕ horns

p. 93

Comprehension

1 ⓒ 2 ⓑ 3 ⓑ
4 ⓒ 5 guitar

6 ⓒ 7 ⓓ 8 ⓔ
9 ⓐ 10 ⓑ

p. 94

Listening Skills Practice: Compare and Contrast I

A ⓐ compare ⓑ compare ⓒ contrast
B

Script

M Teacher: People don't play most of the musical instruments from the Renaissance anymore. Instead, they play more modern versions. Yet a few very old musical instruments have survived to the present day. One is the bagpipe. Another is the hammered dulcimer. The bagpipe has a very unique look. It has a large airtight bag, a melody pipe, and one or more drum pipes. The musician may blow air into the bagpipe or may use a bellows to introduce air into it. Today, the bagpipe is most commonly played in Scotland. It is often played at military funerals and ceremonies. The bagpipe makes a sound unlike any other instrument. Thus most people either love it or hate it. As for the hammered dulcimer, it's a stringed musical instrument. The strings are stretched out over a board. The musician uses two mallets to strike them with. That's where the sound comes from. It makes a sweet sound that people all around the world still enjoy hearing.

1 ⓒ
2 ⓐ
3 ⓐ ⓘⓘⓘ ⓑ ⓘⓘ ⓒ ⓘ

Unit 20 Movie Soundtracks

p. 95

Pre-Listening Questions Sample Answer

1 A movie soundtrack is all of the music that appears in a movie.
2 Classical music appears in many movies. So does rock music.
3 Music can help set the tone in films.
4 I love the *Star Wars* soundtrack. I think that music is great. I also like the *Frozen* soundtrack.

Vocabulary

1 incredibly 2 sadden
3 purpose 4 run
5 talkie 6 suspense

p. 96

Script

W Teacher: Almost all movies have music. The type of music varies. It may be pop songs, rock music, rap, classical music, and even opera. It mostly depends on the genre of the movie. The music doesn't play throughout the entire movie though. Sometimes it plays while it doesn't at other times. Movie directors use music in their films for several purposes. Music can increase the amount of suspense in a film. It can also be used to frighten, sadden, make happy, and amuse viewers. All of the music in a film is called the soundtrack.

The first films ever made were silent movies. Because there was no sound, theaters often played music while the films ran. In many cases, a live pianist or other musicians performed for the viewers. When talkies—movies that had sound—came out in the 1920s, directors began including soundtracks in their films. Since then, the soundtrack has become an integral part of most movies. There are even awards given on a yearly basis for the best film music.

Most movie soundtracks achieve only minor fame. In addition, they sell just a few copies. Others become incredibly famous and sell millions of copies. The soundtrack to *The Sound of Music*, for instance, has sold millions of copies. So too have the soundtracks for the *Star Wars* movies.

Today, there are several individuals who mostly compose film scores. In general, the works they compose are classical in nature. John Williams is probably the best known composer of film scores. Jerry Goldsmith, James Horner, and Ennio Morricone are three other famous film score composers.

Organizer

ⓐ opera ⓑ entire
ⓒ suspense ⓓ amuse
ⓔ millions ⓕ John Williams

p. 97

Comprehension

1 ⓒ 2 ⓐ 3 ⓑ
4 ⓒ 5 *The Sound of Music*

6 ⓓ 7 ⓐ 8 ⓒ
9 ⓔ 10 ⓑ

p. 98

Listening Skills Practice: Compare and Contrast II

A ⓐ Both ⓑ however ⓒ too

B

Script

M Reporter: There is some important news tonight. John Williams, one of the greatest composers of movie soundtracks in history, is going to make a guest appearance with the Boston Pops next month. Williams was the long-time conductor for the Boston Pops in the 1980s and 1990s. Williams is a noted conductor, but he is actually much more famous for his composing. He has written the film scores for nearly all of director Steven Spielberg's movies. Those include *Jaws, Raiders of the Lost Ark*, and *E.T.* In addition, Williams composed the music for the *Star Wars* films. Some of the pieces from *Star Wars* are among the most recognizable of all film music. Williams's soundtracks have sold millions of copies all around the world. He ranks among the bestselling film score composers in history. It is highly likely that tickets for the event will sell out soon. Be sure to make your reservations as soon as you can.

1 ⓑ
2 ⓒ
3 ⓐ yet ⓑ Both ⓒ but

Word List

Word List

Chapter 1 Amazing Animals

Unit 01

1 **behavior** *(n)* the way a person or animal acts
The child's ***behavior*** was poor until his parents made him act better.

2 **captivity** *(n)* custody; the act of not being free
Some animals live long lives in ***captivity***.

3 **communicate** *(v)* to speak with someone else; to talk to another person
We still do not know how to ***communicate*** with most animals.

4 **display** *(v)* to show
The museum will ***display*** some valuable items from Egypt this weekend.

5 **handler** *(n)* a person who takes care of another person or animal
The lion ***handler*** must always be careful around the animals.

6 **humanlike** *(adj)* resembling a human in action or behavior
Some gorillas and chimpanzees can behave in ***humanlike*** ways at times.

7 **mission** *(n)* a goal; an objective
Our ***mission*** is to solve this problem as quickly as possible.

8 **particularly** *(adv)* mostly; mainly
Mr. Jones is ***particularly*** interested in attending medical school.

9 **primate** *(n)* a mammal such as a human, gorilla, or monkey
Many African ***primates*** are endangered species.

10 **researcher** *(n)* a person who does research on a certain topic
Anna is currently working as a ***researcher*** for that company.

Unit 02

1 **allergic** *(adj)* relating to an allergy or an inability to tolerate something
My sister is ***allergic*** to peanut butter, so she cannot eat it.

2 **assist** *(v)* to help; to aid
Could you please ***assist*** me for a few minutes?

3 **disability** *(n)* a handicap; something that prevents a person from living a normal life
Emily has a ***disability*** since she cannot use her right arm.

4 **loneliness** *(n)* a feeling one gets when one is alone
He experienced ***loneliness*** when he went camping by himself for a week.

5 **master** *(n)* an owner, usually of an animal
The dog's ***master*** treats it well and takes good care of it.

6 **miniature** *(adj)* tiny; smaller than normal
This exhibit has several ***miniature*** statues.

7 **press** *(v)* to push
Please ***press*** the button for the tenth floor.

8 **quadriplegic** *(n)* a person who cannot move his or her arms or legs
After the car accident, Karen became a ***quadriplegic***.

9 **relieve** *(v)* to ease; to get rid of stress
What is the best way to ***relieve*** yourself of stress?

10 **wheelchair** *(n)* a chair with wheels used by a person with a disability
Peter has to use a ***wheelchair*** since he broke both of his legs.

Unit 03

1 **aquarium** *(n)* a tank in which fish or other aquatic animals are kept; a large building with many aquatic animals
The students are going to go on a field trip to the local ***aquarium***.

2 **clamp** *(n)* a lock; a hold; a fastener
They put a ***clamp*** on the dog's leg so that it could not run away.

3 **diver** *(n)* a person who swims underwater, often with scuba gear
You need to be able to swim well to be a good ***diver***.

4 **drag** *(v)* to pull
The box was so heavy that I had to ***drag*** it.

5 **guard** *(v)* to protect; to look after
The soldiers will ***guard*** the general as well as they can.

6 **intruder** *(n)* a person who is somewhere that he or she should not be
The police were not able to catch the ***intruder***.

7 **mammal** *(n)* a warm-blooded animal that gives birth to live young and has hair or fur
Mammals are the most dominant animals on the planet today.

8 **mine** *(n)* a bomb that is put in the water and is designed to destroy ships or submarines
The ship sank after it hit a ***mine*** that exploded.

9 **playful** *(adj)* liking to play or to have fun
The kitten is very ***playful*** and enjoys having lots of fun.

10 **positive** *(adj)* sure
Are you ***positive*** that this is the correct answer to the question?

Unit 04

1 **alert** *(v)* to warn
He ***alerted*** the hospital that an emergency patient was going there.

2 **alley** *(n)* a small area in between two buildings
It can be dangerous to go into some ***alleys*** late at night.

3 **announce** *(v)* to state something out loud
We will ***announce*** the winner of the contest soon.

4 **authority** *(n)* a person with power
The government ***authorities*** are behaving in an illegal manner.

5 **breed** *(n)* a specific type of animal, such as a dog or a cat
Most dog ***breeds*** look and act different from one another.

6 **plot** *(n)* a plan
The thieves came up with a ***plot*** to rob the store.

7 **relentless** *(adj)* unwilling to give up; persistent
The ***relentless*** detective did not quit until he had solved the case.

8 **scent** *(n)* a smell; an odor
The dog detected a strange ***scent*** in the room.

9 **sniff** *(v)* to use one's nose to smell something
Why are you ***sniffing*** that package?

10 **suitcase** *(n)* a bag that one takes on a trip; luggage
Be sure to pack your ***suitcase*** before you go to bed tonight.

Chapter 2 Famous Journeys

Unit 05

1 **assistance** *(n)* help; aid
We could use some ***assistance*** right now.

2 **coast** *(n)* the land that is right next to an ocean or sea
They enjoy spending their vacation at the south ***coast*** of the country.

3 **execute** *(v)* to put someone to death
The prisoner was ***executed*** because of the crimes he committed.

4 **explore** *(v)* to look around a new place; to travel; to sightsee
I would like to ***explore*** the jungles of South America.

5 **head** *(v)* to go in a certain direction
Let's ***head*** to the shopping mall later today.

6 **mutiny** *(n)* a rebellion by soldiers or sailors against their leaders
The soldiers were all punished because they attempted a ***mutiny***.

7 **native** *(n)* a person whose home is in a local area
The ***natives*** of this region are very friendly.

8 **reject** *(v)* to turn down; to say no to a person
Jake applied for a job, but the company ***rejected*** him.

9 **rough** *(adj)* hard; difficult
The trip was ***rough*** at first, but then it became much easier.

10 **strait** *(n)* a narrow passage of water that connects two large bodies of water
We must sail through this ***strait*** to get to the ocean.

Unit 06

1 **claim** *(v)* to declare; to state one's belief about something
Kevin ***claimed*** he was right, but he was actually wrong.

2 **confirmed** *(adj)* proven to be true
It was ***confirmed*** that Peter had stolen the money.

3 **desire** *(n)* a wish; an urge
I have a ***desire*** to go on a trip to the beach.

4 **expedition** *(n)* a trip; a voyage
They will go on an ***expedition*** to the desert.

5 **navigational** *(adj)* relating to direction
You really need to improve your ***navigational*** skills.

6 **poor** *(adj)* bad; not good
David got a ***poor*** grade on his test because he did not study.

7 **race** *(n)* a contest of speed
Do you think that you can win the ***race***?

8 **recover** *(v)* to get better; to improve one's health
It will take her about three weeks to ***recover*** from her illness.

9 **sled** *(n)* a vehicle that has skis on the bottom so that it can move on the snow
There is so much snow that people use ***sleds*** to travel.

10 **trek** *(n)* a long, difficult journey
They went on a ten-day ***trek*** through the rainforest.

Unit 07

1 **adventurer** *(n)* a person who likes to travel and to have adventures
The ***adventurers*** will start on their journey in the morning.

2 **canoe** *(n)* a type of boat that is made from a hollowed-out log
It can be difficult to travel in a ***canoe***.

3 **confirm** *(v)* to prove; to show that something is true
Can you ***confirm*** that what you said is the truth?

4 **enlist** *(v)* to join the military
Edward is going to ***enlist*** in the air force next month.

5 **flow** *(v)* to move as a liquid
The water in this river ***flows*** slowly.

6 **paddle** *(v)* to use oars to make a boat move
Do you know how to ***paddle*** a boat to make it move?

7 **realize** *(v)* to recognize that something is true
Jane suddenly ***realized*** that she knew the correct answer.

8 **rumor** *(n)* gossip; a story that may or may not be true; a tale
There is a ***rumor*** that Larry is going to quit his job soon.

9 **superior** *(n)* an employee in a higher position than another; a boss
Your ***superior*** wants to see you in his office right now.

10 **upriver** *(adv)* toward the part of a river that goes to its source
To get to your destination, you must travel ten kilometers ***upriver***.

Unit 08

1 **adventuresome** *(adj)* brave; daring
Doug is an ***adventuresome*** man who likes to have new and exciting experiences.

2 **dense** *(adj)* thick
The trees are very ***dense*** in this part of the forest.

3 **desert** *(v)* suddenly to quit or leave one's job
Soldiers should never ***desert*** and leave their armies.

4 **disease** *(n)* a sickness
The doctors believe Sue caught a ***disease*** while she was traveling.

5 **entire** *(adj)* total; complete
The ***entire*** country is suffering from a drought.

6 **inhospitable** *(adj)* unfriendly; harsh; difficult
The land is so ***inhospitable*** that few people live there.

7 **missionary** *(n)* a person who travels to another place to spread his or her religion
My uncle is a Christian ***missionary*** in South America.

8 **porter** *(n)* a person hired to carry bags for another
They hired several ***porters*** to carry their luggage while they climbed the mountain.

9 **presume** *(v)* to believe; to assume
I ***presume*** that you are telling me the truth.

10 **waterfall** *(n)* flowing water that falls from a higher to a lower place
Victoria Falls is one of the world's most beautiful ***waterfalls***.

Chapter 3 American Folklore

Unit 09

1 **celebrity** *(n)* a famous person
Mark became a ***celebrity*** when he starred in a hit movie.

2 **clash** *(v)* to fight with another person or group
The two men ***clashed*** because they got into an argument.

3 **homeland** *(n)* the country a person is from
David has been away from his ***homeland*** for more than ten years.

4 **kidnap** *(v)* to abduct a person; to take someone away from his or her home
The man tried to ***kidnap*** the child, but another person stopped him.

5 **negotiate** *(v)* to try to come to an agreement with a person
We will ***negotiate*** with the company and try to reach an agreement.

6 **peaceful** *(adj)* nonviolent; passive
The last few years have been a ***peaceful*** time in our country.

7 **territory** *(n)* land that belongs to a country
The country claims a large amount of land as its ***territory***.

8 **trade** *(n)* the exchange of goods and services between two people
The ***trade*** was made after the two sides agreed on the price.

9 **translator** *(n)* a person who interprets from one language to another
Anna wants to become a ***translator*** since she speaks several languages.

10 **trapper** *(n)* a person who catches animals, often for their skins
The ***trapper*** is very interested in catching foxes and beavers.

2 **ax** *(n)* a tool used to cut down trees
Please sharpen your ***ax*** before you try to cut down this tree.

3 **enormous** *(adj)* huge; very large
That forest is so ***enormous*** it will take us five days to hike through it.

4 **folklore** *(n)* traditional stories that are often passed down from one generation to another
We enjoy reading ***folklore*** from many different countries.

5 **lumberjack** *(n)* a person who cuts down trees for a living
The ***lumberjack*** spent more than two hours chopping down a single tree.

6 **mythical** *(adj)* legendary
A roc is a ***mythical*** bird that is as big as an elephant.

7 **orchard** *(n)* an area of land in which people grow fruit or nut trees
He owns a cherry ***orchard*** that has more than twenty cherry trees.

8 **ox** *(n)* a large animal that is like a cow
The farm has one ***ox*** that the farmer uses to do work.

9 **plant** *(v)* to put a seed or small plant into the ground so that it will grow
We will ***plant*** all of the seeds this spring.

10 **simply** *(adv)* modestly; humbly; in a simple way
He lives ***simply*** and has no need for a TV or computer.

Unit 10

1 **apprentice** *(n)* a person who learns a skill from a more knowledgeable person
You must work as an ***apprentice*** for three years to learn everything you need to know.

Unit 11

1 **beneficial** *(adj)* helpful
Eating that fruit will be ***beneficial*** to your health.

2 **dreadful** *(adj)* terrible; awful; very bad
The movie was ***dreadful***, so nobody enjoyed it.

3 **escape** *(v)* to get away from someone or something

The dog ***escaped*** from its pen and ran away.

4 **feast** *(n)* an event at which there is a lot of food for people to eat

We will have a ***feast*** and will serve all kinds of food there.

5 **harmful** *(adj)* dangerous

That liquid is ***harmful***, so please do not drink it.

6 **harvest** *(n)* the crops that are gathered from fields

The farmer had a record ***harvest*** of corn and wheat this year.

7 **provide** *(v)* to deliver; to give

I can ***provide*** you with money if you need to borrow some.

8 **sap** *(n)* a thick, sticky liquid that comes from trees

The ***sap*** of the maple tree can be turned into maple syrup.

9 **slave** *(n)* a person who is owned by another

Some people in the Middle East still own ***slaves*** today.

10 **surprise** *(v)* to shock; to do something that another person is not expecting

It ***surprised*** Ken when he got an A on his report.

Unit 12

1 **besiege** *(v)* to surround a place in order to attack the people in it

The army ***besieged*** the city for more than three months.

2 **declare** *(v)* to state that something is true

Eric ***declared*** that he was going to run for president.

3 **defender** *(n)* a person who is protecting a place

The ***defenders*** promised to protect the people they were guarding.

4 **develop** *(v)* to form; to create

Let's ***develop*** a plan for the future.

5 **displeased** *(adj)* unhappy

The teacher was ***displeased*** with the essay that Mary wrote.

6 **hostile** *(adj)* unfriendly

Some tribes in the jungle are ***hostile*** to outsiders.

7 **independence** *(adj)* freedom

The people want their ***independence*** from the oppressive government.

8 **legend** *(n)* a story from the past that may or may not be true; a myth

She enjoys reading the ***legends*** of King Arthur.

9 **roughly** *(adv)* about; around

It will take us ***roughly*** forty minutes to arrive at your house.

10 **seek** *(v)* to look for

I am ***seeking*** a job in the manufacturing industry.

Chapter 4 Historical Mysteries

Unit 13

1 **archaeologist** *(n)* a person who studies people and cultures from the past

Indiana Jones is the name of an ***archaeologist*** in some movies.

2 **capture** *(v)* to catch

We are going into the forest to try to ***capture*** some rabbits.

3 **carve** *(v)* to cut with a knife

Use the big knife to ***carve*** the turkey.

4 **found** *(v)* to start a group or organization; to establish

Mr. Simmons ***founded*** the hospital in 1986.

5 **governor** *(n)* the elected representative of a group of people

The ***governor*** was unpopular, so he lost the next election.

6 **historian** *(n)* a person who studies the past

My brother wants to be a ***historian*** in the future.

7 **legion** *(n)* a Roman army

The ***legion*** defeated the barbarian army it fought.

8 **prisoner** *(n)* a person who has been captured by another

The ***prisoner*** had to spend more than three years in jail.

9 **shield** *(n)* a wide piece of armor a person holds with his or her arm to use for defense

The knight used his ***shield*** to block the sword his opponent was using.

10 **unearth** *(v)* to dig up from out of the ground

The diggers ***unearthed*** some coins that were a thousand years old.

Unit 14

1 **abduct** *(v)* to kidnap

The kidnappers ***abducted*** several children until the police caught them.

2 **accomplish** *(v)* to do; to be successful

Can you ***accomplish*** the task by tomorrow morning?

3 **bracelet** *(n)* a type of jewelry worn on the wrist

Jenny's mother gave her a gold ***bracelet*** for her birthday.

4 **expert** *(n)* a person who knows a great deal about a certain subject

Tim is an ***expert*** on military history.

5 **interrupt** *(v)* to disturb; to bother

Please do not ***interrupt*** me when I am speaking.

6 **mystery** *(n)* something that is unknown

There are many unsolved ***mysteries*** all around the world.

7 **pilot** *(n)* a person who can fly an airplane or helicopter

It takes many hours of practice before you can become a ***pilot***.

8 **recover** *(v)* to get something back

The bank is trying to ***recover*** the stolen money.

9 **vanish** *(v)* to disappear

The strange lights suddenly ***vanished*** from the sky.

10 **wrecked** *(adj)* crashed

We saw a ***wrecked*** car on the side of the road.

Unit 15

1 **access** *(n)* entry; admission

It costs five dollars to gain ***access*** to the museum.

2 **alien** *(n)* a being from another world

Some people believe that ***aliens*** exist.

3 **artifact** *(n)* an object

We found some ***artifacts*** from the past while we were digging in the backyard.

4 **civilian** *(n)* anyone who is not in the military

Many ***civilians*** are upset with the quality of the politicians these days.

5 **destruction** *(n)* downfall; ruin

The ***destruction*** of the city happened for several reasons.

6 **official** *(adj)* approved; legal

This is the ***official*** form that you must fill out to get your driver's license.

7 **precious** *(adj)* valuable

Tina's most ***precious*** possession is a doll she had as a child.

8 **purpose** *(n)* a use

What is the ***purpose*** of this object here?

9 **spacecraft** *(n)* a vehicle that can fly in outer space

The engineers want to build a ***spacecraft*** that can fly to the stars.

10 **vast** *(adj)* very large; huge; enormous

There is a ***vast*** amount of oil underneath the world's oceans.

Unit 16

1 **abandon** *(v)* to leave behind; to give up

They ***abandoned*** their home when it burned down.

2 **airman** *(n)* a person who works on an airplane, helicopter, or other flying vehicle

There are five ***airmen*** on that plane.

3 **cargo** *(n)* all of the items that a vehicle such as an airplane or ship is carrying

The men are busy loading all of the ***cargo*** onto the ship.

4 **crewman** *(n)* a person who works on a ship

The captain gave his ***crewmen*** some orders to follow.

5 **depart** *(v)* to go away; to leave

We plan to ***depart*** for the airport at one in the afternoon.

6 **graveyard** *(n)* a place where many people are buried

His grandparents are buried in the ***graveyard*** beside the church.

7 **onboard** *(adj)* on a vehicle such as an airplane or ship

Most of the passengers are already ***onboard***.

8 **possession** *(n)* an item that a person has or owns

Julie's favorite ***possession*** is her smartphone.

9 **theory** *(n)* an idea; a hypothesis

The scientists have a ***theory*** about the origins of the universe.

10 **valuable** *(n)* an item that is worth a lot to a person

Put all of your ***valuables*** in a safe place.

Chapter 5 Music

Unit 17

1 **album** *(n)* a collection of songs

My brother gave me a rock ***album*** for my birthday.

2 **award** *(n)* a prize

Mark won an ***award*** at the school's science fair.

3 **awe** *(v)* to amaze someone

Rick ***awed*** everyone with his athletic ability.

4 **debut** *(n)* a start; a beginning

Since Janet's ***debut*** last month, she has been famous.

5 **famed** *(adj)* famous; well-known

They are going to have dinner at the ***famed*** restaurant by the river.

6 **incredible** *(adj)* amazing

It is ***incredible*** that men have visited the moon.

7 **numerous** *(adj)* great in number; very many

There are ***numerous*** ways to solve this problem.

8 **popularize** *(v)* to make something liked or popular with others

She helped ***popularize*** the sport of volleyball in her country.

9 **quartet** *(n)* a group of four people

John is a member of a singing ***quartet***.

10 **recognize** *(v)* to know who someone or something is

I cannot ***recognize*** any of the people in the picture.

Unit 18

1 **audience** *(n)* a group of people watching a performance
The ***audience*** gave the singer a standing ovation at the end of the show.

2 **compose** *(v)* to write a work of music or literature
It took Jack three days to ***compose*** his newest song.

3 **create** *(v)* to make; to produce
Can you ***create*** a work of art in a short time?

4 **harpsichord** *(n)* an old keyboard instrument that was similar to a piano
Pam learned to play the ***harpsichord*** at college.

5 **hire** *(v)* to give a person a job; to employ a person
The company plans to ***hire*** three new employees this week.

6 **masterpiece** *(n)* a great work of art
Tim considers this painting to be his ***masterpiece***.

7 **oratorio** *(n)* a dramatic work of music in which an orchestra and singers perform but do not act
They will see a performance of an ***oratorio*** tonight.

8 **patron** *(n)* a person who sponsors another, often to produce art of some kind
Mr. Thompson is a ***patron*** of the arts who sponsors several painters and writers.

9 **resurrection** *(n)* the act of coming back to life after being dead
The ***resurrection*** of Jesus Christ is an important part of Christianity.

10 **touched** *(adj)* impressed; moved
I was ***touched*** by his act of kindness in helping the old couple.

Unit 19

1 **bellows** *(n)* a device that can produce blowing air
The blacksmith used the ***bellows*** to make the fire hotter.

2 **bow** *(n)* a long, thin stick used to play some stringed instruments
Pull the ***bow*** across the string to make a sound.

3 **ceremony** *(n)* a special event held in honor of someone or something
We will have a ***ceremony*** for the new employees tomorrow.

4 **evolve** *(v)* to change over time; to adapt
Many animals have ***evolved*** over time.

5 **funeral** *(n)* an event held when a person dies
Many people attended her grandfather's ***funeral***.

6 **mallet** *(n)* a small hammer
The musician hit the drum with a ***mallet***.

7 **melody** *(n)* a tune
A nice ***melody*** is playing on the radio.

8 **modern** *(adj)* current; contemporary; present-day
Life has improved greatly in the ***modern*** age.

9 **stretch** *(v)* to pull both sides of something as far as possible
Do not ***stretch*** the cloth too far, or it will tear in half.

10 **sweet** *(adj)* pleasant
The roses in the garden give off a ***sweet*** smell.

Unit 20

1 **appearance** *(n)* an arrival; an entrance; the act of going somewhere
The famous soccer player made an ***appearance*** at the theater.

2 **bestselling** *(adj)* selling very well; selling better than most other similar things
Thanks to his ***bestselling*** novels, he became a wealthy man.

3 **composer** *(n)* a person who writes a work of music

The ***composer*** hopes to finish his work by next month.

4 **conductor** *(n)* a person who leads a band or orchestra

The musicians are waiting for the ***conductor*** to arrive.

5 **reservation** *(n)* a booking; the purchasing of a ticket in advance

Please make a ***reservation*** so that we will have plane tickets

6 **sadden** *(v)* to make someone unhappy or sad

He was ***saddened*** to see the poor children.

7 **score** *(n)* a work of music for a film or play

The musicians are trying to learn to play the ***score***.

8 **soundtrack** *(n)* a collection of music played in a film or play

He loves listening to the ***soundtracks*** of his favorite movies.

9 **talkie** *(n)* a movie in which there is sound

The first ***talkies*** appeared in the 1920s.

10 **yearly** *(adj)* once a year; every year

Sue's family takes a ***yearly*** trip to the beach in July.

memo

memo

A Guide to Mastering Listening Skills for Academic Lectures

Mastering Listening Skills

Michael A. Putlack

2

Workbook

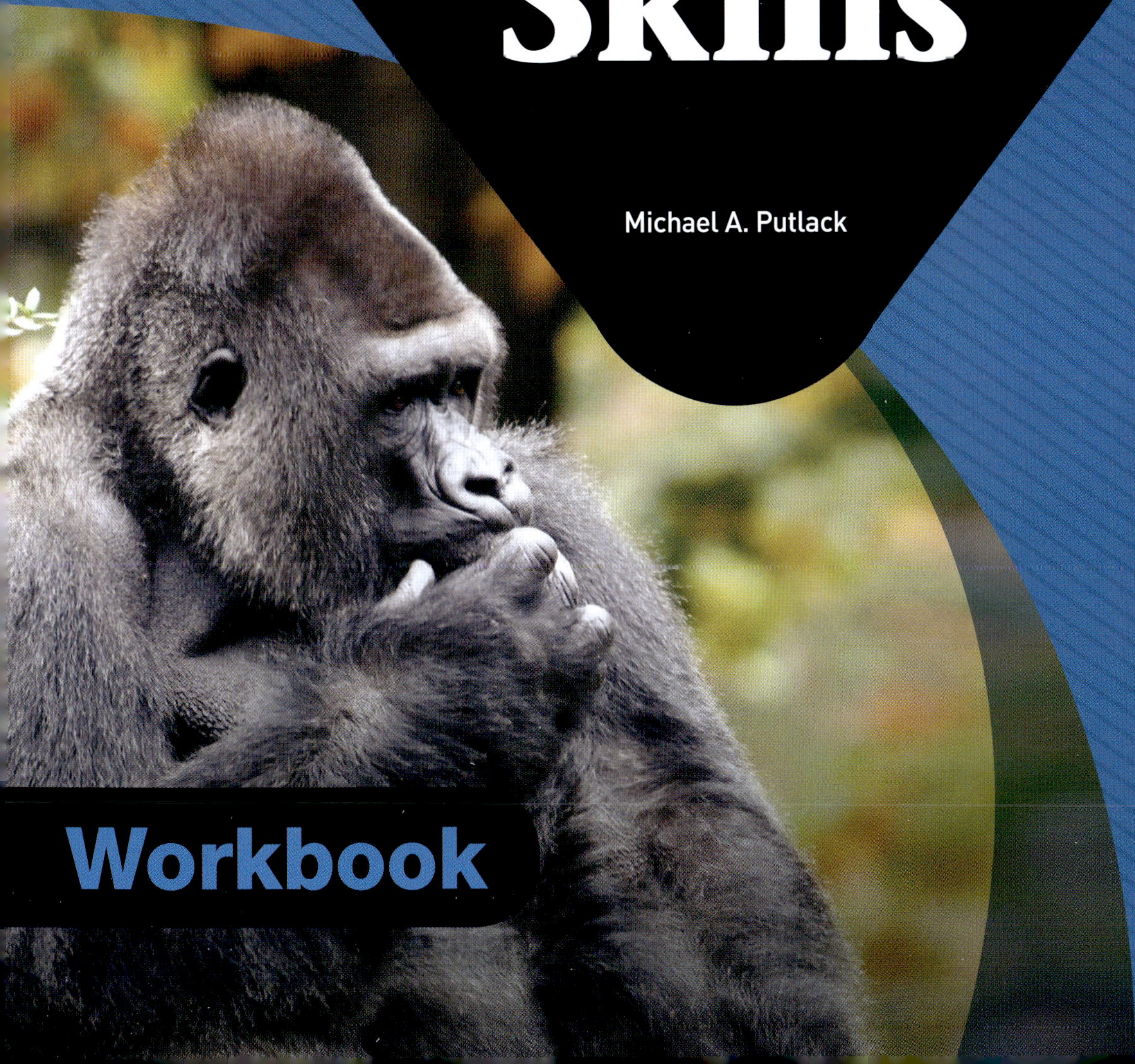

DARAKWON

Mastering Listening Skills

Workbook

2

DARAKWON

Chapter

1

Amazing Animals

Unit 01

Koko the Gorilla

A Listen to the talk on page 12 again. Then, write the answers to the questions.

1 Which animals did scientists believe they could teach to communicate with humans?

____

2 Where was Koko born?

____

3 What was the mission of the Gorilla Foundation?

____

4 How many signs does Koko know?

____

5 What are some of the pets Koko has owned?

____

B Use the words in the box to complete the sentences. You may need to change the forms of the words.

to some extent	display	tame animal	nonhuman	be involved in

1 That dog is a ________________, so it will not bite you.

2 Can you please ________________ your new invention for us?

3 Eagles and deer are two animals that are ________________.

4 Jason has learned how to swim ________________.

5 Sally ________________ a large number of activities at school.

C Listen to the talk on page 14 again. Then, fill in the blanks with the correct words.

1 Both gorillas and ________________ have learned to communicate with sign language.

2 The first ________________ to learn sign language was named Washoe.

3 Washoe learned around ________________ in American Sign Language.

4 Washoe enjoyed looking through ________________ catalogs.

5 Washoe taught the chimp Louis his first ________________ soon after she met him.

D Listen to the talk. Then, choose the main idea.

Notes

ⓐ Some animals have actually learned to speak human language as well.

ⓑ Parrots can learn to speak some words that humans say.

ⓒ Other more unusual animals have learned to speak certain languages.

Unit 02

Seeing-Eye Dogs

A **Listen to the talk on page 16 again. Then, write the answers to the questions.**

1 What do blind people often use when they walk?

____

2 Which breed of dogs were the first seeing-eye dogs?

____

3 What must dogs be like to become seeing-eye dogs?

____

4 How do dogs learn to become seeing-eye dogs?

____

5 What often happens to seeing-eye dogs and their owners?

____

B **Use the words in the box to complete the sentences. You may need to change the forms of the words.**

function	train	in good health	sidewalk	run into

1 We need to ____________ the new employee how to use the computer.

2 People should always walk on the ____________ instead of in the road.

3 Be careful while you are walking, or you might ____________ someone.

4 To ____________ in society, you need to have good manners.

5 Susan is ____________ since she exercises regularly and eats nutritious food.

C Listen to the talk on page 18 again. Then, answer T (true) or F (false).

1 ______ Miniature horses are the most common types of service animals.

2 ______ Miniature horses can live indoors with people.

3 ______ People who are allergic to dog hair often use miniature horses.

4 ______ Monkeys are not very good with their hands.

5 ______ Service monkeys can talk on the phone for their masters.

D Listen to the talk. Then, choose the main idea.

Notes

ⓐ They can also forms close bonds with humans.

ⓑ Eventually, a man stopped his car when he saw LuLu.

ⓒ Thanks to LuLu's quick thinking, her owner didn't die that day.

Unit 03

Military Dolphins

A Listen to the talk on page 20 again. Then, write the answers to the questions.

1 Who do the two dolphins find in the water?

____

2 Why did the U.S. military start studying dolphins?

____

3 How smart are dolphins?

____

4 What can dolphins detect?

____

5 In which three wars did dolphins helps the U.S. Navy?

____

B Use the words in the box to complete the sentences. You may need to change the forms of the words.

go off	scuba gear	aircraft carrier	interact	retrieve

1 I like to throw a ball and to let my dog ______________ it.

2 The bomb is set to ______________ in about five minutes.

3 An ______________ can hold more than fifty airplanes and helicopters.

4 Thanks to ______________, people can swim underwater for a long time.

5 The students and teachers ______________ well with one another.

C Listen to the talk on page 22 again. Then, circle the correct answers.

1 The California sea lion has (two / four) flippers.

2 The California sea lion is a very (playful / serious) animal.

3 The U.S. Navy uses sea lions to protect its ships from (submarines / divers).

4 The sea lions learn to swim (ahead of / behind) the enemy in the water.

5 The sea lions can attach a (rope / chain) to the enemy's leg.

D Listen to the talk. Then, write F (fact) or O (opinion) in each blank.

Notes

1 ______ Nowadays, militaries use animals such as dolphins, sea lions, and dogs.

2 ______ I think it was very clever of people to use the birds this way.

3 ______ Several armies used homing pigeons in World War I and World War II.

Unit 04 Bloodhounds

A Listen to the talk on page 24 again. Then, write the answers to the questions.

1 Where did the bloodhound find the murderer?

____

2 How does the teacher feel about bloodhounds?

____

3 How can bloodhounds' curiosity cause problems?

____

4 What do bloodhounds do when they pick up a scent?

____

5 How many criminals did one bloodhound help convict?

____

B Use the words in the box to complete the sentences. You may need to change the forms of the words.

jail	recapture	pick up	track down	wander off

1 The man has to spend three years in ______________ for robbing the store.

2 The bloodhound is trying to ______________ the escaped criminal.

3 Do not ______________, or you might get lost.

4 The police need to ______________ the thief since she escaped last night.

5 The animals could not ______________ the scent, so the person got away.

C Listen to the talk on page 26 again. Then, choose the correct answers.

1 There was a terrorist plot to destroy ________________.

ⓐ a train ⓑ an airplane ⓒ a bus

2 A passenger had a ________________ with a bomb in it.

ⓐ suitcase ⓑ box ⓒ carry-on bag

3 A dog named ________________ found the bomb.

ⓐ Friday ⓑ Snowy ⓒ Rusty

4 The ________________ arrived and took the bomb apart.

ⓐ military ⓑ FBI ⓒ bomb squad

5 The police ________________ the man who had the bomb.

ⓐ shot ⓑ beat up ⓒ arrested

D Listen to the talk. Then, write F (fact) or O (opinion) in each blank.

Notes

1 ______ That's a wise decision since German shepherds are big, powerful, and intelligent.

2 ______ Other times, police use them to detect bombs, drugs, or other illegal substances.

3 ______ K-9s and their trainers often work closely together for many years.

Chapter

2

Famous Journeys

Unit 05

Ferdinand Magellan

A Listen to the talk on page 30 again. Then, write the answers to the questions.

1 Where did Ferdinand Magellan sail to when he was a young man?

____

2 Who provided money for Ferdinand Magellan to sail across the Atlantic Ocean?

____

3 How many ships did Ferdinand Magellan prepare?

____

4 Where was Ferdinand Magellan killed?

____

5 How many sailors survived the trip around the world?

____

B Use the words in the box to complete the sentences. You may need to change the forms of the words.

agree	run out of	journey	tip	survivor

1 We are going to ______________ food soon, so let's go to the supermarket.

2 They will sail south around the ______________ of Africa and then sail north.

3 There was only one ______________ in the car crash.

4 The ______________ across the country will take a couple of days.

5 Peter ______________ to help Mary since she asked him nicely.

C Listen to the talk on page 32 again. Then, fill in the blanks with the correct words.

1 The water in the Strait of Magellan is very ________________.

2 The Europeans looked for other ways to get into the ________________.

3 Giovanni de Verrazano was ________________ but sailed for the French.

4 Giovanni de Verrazano started exploring the North American coast at ________________.

5 Giovanni de Verrazano sailed into ________________ and met some Native Americans.

D Listen to the talk. Then, put the sentences in the correct order.

Notes

1 ______ Henry Hudson sailed into Hudson Bay.

2 ______ Henry Hudson sailed east to Russia.

3 ______ Henry Hudson discovered the Hudson River.

Unit 06

Roald Amundsen

A Listen to the talk on page 34 again. Then, write the answers to the questions.

1 What did Roald Amundsen search for on his first adventure?

____

2 Where did Roald Amundsen arrive in 1911?

____

3 What was Roald Amundsen's goal on his second adventure?

____

4 How did Roald Amundsen get to the North Pole?

____

5 How did Roald Amundsen die?

____

B Use the words in the box to complete the sentences. You may need to change the forms of the words.

set one's sights on	polar region	hometown	latter	team up with

1 The Earth's ________ are among the coldest places on the planet.

2 Of the two songs we heard, I prefer the ________.

3 Jason is going to ________ George and Sam to do the project with them.

4 David has ________ becoming a doctor before he turns twenty-seven.

5 Clara lives in London, but her ________ is Dublin, Ireland.

C Listen to the talk on page 36 again. Then, answer T (true) or F (false).

1 ______ Frederick Cook claimed he went to the North Pole in 1908.

2 ______ Most people believed that Robert Peary made it to the North Pole.

3 ______ Richard Byrd said he flew over the North Pole in an airplane.

4 ______ Richard Byrd's journey took fewer hours than expected.

5 ______ Roald Amundsen was the second man to visit the North Pole.

D Listen to the talk. Then, put the sentences in the correct order.

Notes

1 ______ Richard Byrd claimed he had flown over the North Pole.

2 ______ Richard Byrd flew his plane over the South Pole.

3 ______ Charles Lindbergh made a nonstop transatlantic flight.

Unit 07

Captain Cook

A Listen to the talk on page 38 again. Then, write the answers to the questions.

1 Where did James Cook grow up?

____

2 What was James Cook good at drawing?

____

3 Where did James Cook visit on his first great expedition?

____

4 What was James Cook looking for on his second great expedition?

____

5 Where did James Cook go on his third great expedition?

____

B Use the words in the box to complete the sentences. You may need to change the forms of the words.

agriculture	islander	merchant ship	be fascinated by	end the life of

1 The ______________ is loaded with all kinds of trade goods.

2 People have been practicing ______________ for thousands of years.

3 The murderer ______________ of the good man that he killed.

4 The ______________ has no desire to go to the mainland but wants to stay in Hawaii.

5 The young child ______________ the animated movie she was watching.

C Listen to the talk on page 40 again. Then, circle the correct answers.

1 The Mississippi River is the greatest river in (North / South) America.

2 The Mississippi River empties into the (Gulf of Mexico / Atlantic Ocean).

3 Marquette and Joliet used (rafts / canoes) to go down the Mississippi River.

4 Marquette and Joliet met some (Native Americans / Frenchmen) on their journey.

5 Marquette and Joliet returned north so that they could avoid the (Spaniards / Italians).

D Listen to the talk. Then, circle the words that the speaker stresses.

Notes

1 He also became the first man since the Vikings to set foot on the North American mainland.

2 Then, he claimed all of the land there for England.

3 However, the British would not establish any permanent colonies in North America for more than 100 years.

Unit 08

Stanley and Livingstone

A **Listen to the talk on page 42 again. Then, write the answers to the questions.**

1 What is the northern part of Africa like?

____

2 What did David Livingstone discover?

____

3 Why did Henry Morgan Stanley go to Africa?

____

4 How far did Henry Morgan Stanley travel in Africa?

____

5 What did Henry Morgan Stanley say when he saw Dr. Livingstone?

____

B **Use the words in the box to complete the sentences. You may need to change the forms of the words.**

utter	surrounded by	interior	desert	transcontinental journey

1 The farmer's field are ________________ fences.

2 There is little water in the ________________, so you need to be cautious there.

3 Our ________________ will take us from the Atlantic Ocean to the Pacific Ocean.

4 Please do not ________________ a word until you hear the entire presentation.

5 I really like how you decorated the ________________ of this building.

C Listen to the talk on page 44 again. Then, choose the correct answers.

1 Hendri Coetzee was killed by a __________.

ⓐ snake ⓑ crocodile ⓒ hippopotamus

2 Hendri Coetzee was exploring the __________ River when he was killed.

ⓐ Lukuga ⓑ Niger ⓒ Nile

3 Hendri Coetzee often went over waterfalls in __________.

ⓐ canoes ⓑ barrels ⓒ boats

4 In 2004, Hendri Coetzee started an expedition at __________ in Tanzania.

ⓐ Lake Victoria ⓑ the Serengeti ⓒ Victoria Falls

5 On May 21, Hendri Coetzee became the first person to sail the entire length of the __________.

ⓐ Mediterranean Sea ⓑ Nile River ⓒ Red Sea

D Listen to the talk. Then, circle the words that the speaker stresses.

Notes

1 I guarantee you're going to have the trip of a lifetime.

2 This is going to be the most incredible tour.

3 And, of course, you'll see all kinds of wildlife in the river itself.

Chapter

3

American Folklore

Unit 09

Pocahontas

A Listen to the talk on page 48 again. Then, write the answers to the questions.

1 Who was the leader of the Jamestown colonists?

____

2 Why were many of the Indians unfriendly to the colonists?

____

3 Who was Powhatan?

____

4 How did Pocahontas help the colonists?

____

5 Who did Pocahontas marry?

____

B Use the words in the box to complete the sentences. You may need to change the forms of the words.

captivity	beat to death	hostile	harsh	execute

1 The angry crowd ______________ the criminal ______________ when they caught him.

2 The land in the desert is ______________ because there is no water.

3 They will ______________ the man who murdered several people.

4 Some animals do not live well when they are in ______________.

5 Anna was ______________ to the new worker after the two had an argument.

C Listen to the talk on page 50 again. Then, fill in the blanks with the correct words.

1 Lewis and Clark explored the ________________.

2 Sacajawea was a member of the ________________ tribe.

3 Toussaint Charbonneau was the ________________ of Sacajawea.

4 Sacajawea was a ________________, so she talked to other tribes.

5 The Lewis and Clark expedition was a ________________ thanks to Sacajawea.

D Listen to the talk. Practice dictation by writing the exact words the speaker says.

Notes

1 His mother was a Cherokee while ____.

2 However, the Cherokee tribe ____.

3 They even started ____ after just a few years.

Unit 10

Johnny Appleseed

A Listen to the talk on page 52 again. Then, write the answers to the questions.

1 What are three states in the American Midwest?

____

2 What was Johnny Appleseed's real name?

____

3 How did Johnny Appleseed learn about apples?

____

4 What did Johnny Appleseed do with the apple trees he took care of?

____

5 What did Johnny Appleseed wear?

____

B Use the words in the box to complete the sentences. You may need to change the forms of the words.

respect	take care of	cloth sack	colorful character	figure

1 Children should always ________________ their parents.

2 A ________________ is a person who has a unique personality.

3 The babysitter will ________________ of the children while their parents are away.

4 The president of that country is one of the world's most powerful ________________.

5 You can put all of the items in that ________________.

C Listen to the talk on page 54 again. Then, answer T (true) or F (false).

1 ______ Paul Bunyan was a Canadian lumberjack.

2 ______ Lumberjacks are people who cut down trees.

3 ______ Paul Bunyan had an ox named Babe.

4 ______ According to legends, Babe created the Grand Canyon.

5 ______ People said that Paul Bunyan created the Great Lakes.

D Listen to the talk. Practice dictation by writing the exact words the speaker says.

Notes

1 These lands were ______________________________ to live in.

2 According to the stories, he was ______________________________.

3 Thanks to these stories, Pecos Bill is ______________________________.

Unit 11

The First Thanksgiving

A **Listen to the talk on page 56 again. Then, write the answers to the questions.**

1 Where in America did the Pilgrims land?

____

2 Who was the Indian that greeted the Pilgrims in English?

____

3 How was the first harvest for the Pilgrims?

____

4 How many Indians showed up for the feast?

____

5 When do Americans celebrate Thanksgiving today?

____

B **Use the words in the box to complete the sentences. You may need to change the forms of the words.**

show up	celebrate	set sail	national holiday	all kinds of

1 We are going to _______________ winning the championship with a pizza party.

2 Christmas is a _______________ in many countries around the world.

3 At the local supermarket, you can purchase _______________ different foods.

4 What time should I _______________ for work tomorrow?

5 The ship will _______________ in a couple of hours.

C Listen to the talk on page 58 again. Then, circle the correct answers.

1 Squanto was a member of the (Cherokee / Patuxet) tribe.

2 In 1614, Squanto left America and went to (Canada / Spain).

3 When Squanto returned to his tribe, most of them had died of (smallpox / polio).

4 Squanto went to meet the Pilgrims because he spoke (English / French) well.

5 Thanks to Squanto, the Pilgrims survived their first (harvest / year).

D Listen to the talk. Then, read a part of the talk and guess the meaning of the underlined word.

Notes

Wolf is gone, so he walks to his village by himself. He doesn't <u>recognize</u> anyone. Rip learns that he slept for more than twenty years.

ⓐ know
ⓑ meet
ⓒ like

Unit 12

Davy Crockett

A **Listen to the talk on page 60 again. Then, write the answers to the questions.**

1 Where was Davey Crockett born?

____

2 Why did Davey Crockett run away from home?

____

3 Why did Davey Crockett get involved in politics?

____

4 Why did Davey Crockett leave Washington, D.C.?

____

5 What happened to Davey Crockett at the Alamo?

____

B **Use the words in the box to complete the sentences. You may need to change the forms of the words.**

frontiersman	be hard on	coonskin cap	legislature	spokesperson

1 Paul's father ________________ him when he was growing up.

2 Several members of the ________________ were arrested for breaking the law.

3 The hunter always wears a ________________ when he is in the forest.

4 He is a ________________ who enjoys spending time out in the wilderness.

5 The reporters asked the company ________________ some questions.

C **Listen to the talk on page 62 again. Then, choose the correct answers.**

1 The Alamo was originally a _______________ mission and school.

ⓐ Texan ⓑ Mexican ⓒ Spanish

2 The leader of the Mexican army was _______________.

ⓐ Don Juan ⓑ Santa Anna ⓒ Pancho Villa

3 There were around _______________ men defending the Alamo.

ⓐ 20 ⓑ 200 ⓒ 2,000

4 Many great _______________ died at the Alamo.

ⓐ Spaniards ⓑ Mexicans ⓒ Texans

5 The Texan battle cry became "_______________ the Alamo."

ⓐ Don't forget ⓑ Fight for ⓒ Remember

D **Listen to the talk. Then, read a part of the talk and guess the meaning of the underlined word.**

Notes

However, he had to cross the Appalachian Mountains. Boone <u>discovered</u> the Cumberland Gap. It was a narrow pass through the mountains to Kentucky.

ⓐ invented

ⓑ made

ⓒ located

C h a p t e r

4

Historical Mysteries

Unit 13

The Lost Colony of Roanoke

A Listen to the talk on page 66 again. Then, write the answers to the questions.

1 What was the first permanent English colony in North America?

____

2 Where is Roanoke Island located?

____

3 What was the name of the first English child born in North America?

____

4 What did John White do after the child was born?

____

5 What was the word carved into a tree that John White found?

____

B Use the words in the box to complete the sentences. You may need to change the forms of the words.

to this day	attempt	ruins	get along with	go back

1 Please do not ______________ to open the door since it is locked.

2 Mary and Kate ______________ each other well these days.

3 Let's ______________ home because it is going to rain soon.

4 Nobody has solved the mystery ______________.

5 There are ______________ of many ancient buildings in Rome.

C Listen to the talk on page 68 again. Then, fill in the blanks with the correct words.

1 A Roman army lost the ________________ in 53 B.C.

2 ________________ wonder what happened to the soldiers who were taken prisoner.

3 A Chinese ________________ wrote about the way some soldiers fought by using their shields.

4 Archaeologists digging in Zhelaizhai have found Roman ________________ and pottery.

5 Some of the ________________ the archaeologists found have Western features.

D Listen to the talk. Then, read a part of the talk and choose the correct paraphrase.

Notes

> There are several theories about what happened to the Roanoke colonists. Many people believe the local Indians killed all of the colonists. But lots of people think the colonists survived.

ⓐ It is highly likely that local Indians killed all of the colonists living on Roanoke Island.
ⓑ Some Indians in America learned to speak English and also became Christians.
ⓒ People have come up with various theories about what happened to the Roanoke colonists.

Unit 14 Amelia Earhart

A **Listen to the talk on page 70 again. Then, write the answers to the questions.**

1 When did Amelia Earhart see her first airplane?

____

2 When did Amelia Earhart fly solo across the Atlantic Ocean?

____

3 Who was Fred Noonan?

____

4 How far did Amelia Earhart make it on her trip around the world?

____

5 What do most people believe happened to Amelia Earhart?

____

B **Use the words in the box to complete the sentences. You may need to change the forms of the words.**

feat	desert island	airshow	spy	decade

1 At the ______________, there are many different kinds of planes on display.

2 David stopped working and traveled around the world for a ______________.

3 When the ship sank, the survivors swam to a ______________ and stayed there.

4 The police caught the ______________ trying to steal the documents.

5 It was an amazing ______________ when John set the world record.

C Listen to the talk on page 72 again. Then, answer T (true) or F (false).

1 ______ The French found the missing plane flown by Antoine de Saint-Exupery.

2 ______ Antoine de Saint-Exupery wrote the book *The Little Prince*.

3 ______ In 1998, a diver found a bracelet with Saint-Exupery's name on it.

4 ______ In 2004, a fisherman located the plane in the water.

5 ______ No one has found Antoine de Saint-Exupery's body yet.

D Listen to the talk. Then, read a part of the talk and choose the correct paraphrase.

Notes

On March 10, 1956, a Broken Arrow involving a U.S. Air Force plane happened. The plane was a B-47 bomber. It took off from the United States and was flying to Morocco. It had to cross the Atlantic Ocean. Sadly, the plane never arrived.

ⓐ A Broken Arrow happens when a nuclear weapon or nuclear material is lost.
ⓑ A U.S. Air Force plane suffered a Broken Arrow in 1956, but it was never found.
ⓒ The U.S. military tried to find the plane that crashed, but the search was unsuccessful.

Unit 15

Atlantis

A **Listen to the talk on page 74 again. Then, write the answers to the questions.**

1 Who were the founders of Atlantis?

____

2 What was in the center of Atlantis?

____

3 Who told the story of Atlantis more than 2,300 years ago?

____

4 Where are some possible locations of Atlantis?

____

5 Why do some people continue to search for Atlantis?

____

B **Use the words in the box to complete the sentences. You may need to change the forms of the words.**

proof	make up	exotic animal	point out	exist

1 Some people think ghosts ______________, but others do not.

2 The elephant is an ______________ that only lives in some places on the Earth.

3 You need to have ______________ that he stole the money before you call the police.

4 The tour guide is going to ______________ all of the important sites.

5 John is able to ______________ funny and creative stories all of the time.

C Listen to the talk on page 76 again. Then, circle the correct answers.

1 Groom Lake is located near (Las Vegas / Los Angeles).

2 (Area 15 / Area 51) is the name most people call Groom Lake.

3 Some people think the U.S. military (tests weapons / fights aliens) at Groom Lake.

4 A few people claim they have seen (spaceships / aliens) at Groom Lake.

5 It is impossible for (soldiers / civilians) to get near Groom Lake.

D Listen to the talk. Then, match the sentences to complete the supporting details.

Notes

1 There are ruins in the

2 The Canary Islands are

3 Ruins more than 9,000 years

ⓐ located near Morocco.

ⓑ old are on Malta.

ⓒ waters around Bimini Island.

Unit 16

The Bermuda Triangle

A Listen to the talk on page 78 again. Then, write the answers to the questions.

1 What three places connect to make the Bermuda Triangle?

____

2 How many ships and planes have disappeared in the Bermuda Triangle in the past 500 years?

____

3 What happened to the *U.S.S. Cyclops*?

____

4 What happened to Flight 19?

____

5 What happened to the planes that were sent out to rescue Flight 19?

____

B Use the words in the box to complete the sentences. You may need to change the forms of the words.

clear weather	without a trace	crash	naval base	triangle

1 The bank robbers stole the money and disappeared ______________.

2 There are two aircraft carriers and many ships at the ______________ right now.

3 There is ______________ today, so we should go on a picnic.

4 It takes three lines to draw a ______________.

5 You will ______________ the car if you drive too fast.

C Listen to the talk on page 80 again. Then, choose the correct answers.

1 People say that the *Mary Celeste* was a ________________ ship.

ⓐ ghost ⓑ pirate ⓒ lucky

2 The *Mary Celeste* departed from ________________ in 1872.

ⓐ New York ⓑ Miami ⓒ Italy

3 Another ship found the *Mary Celeste*, but ________________ was aboard.

ⓐ only the captain ⓑ one sailor ⓒ no one

4 The sailors' valuables and the ship's ________________ were still on the ship.

ⓐ papers ⓑ cargo ⓒ equipment

5 Some people say that ________________ abducted the people on the *Mary Celeste*.

ⓐ soldiers ⓑ aliens ⓒ pirates

D Listen to the talk. Then, write MI (main idea) or SD (supporting detail).

Notes

1 ______ The captain put some crew members on the other ship.

2 ______ The ship disappeared in the middle of a storm.

3 ______ The *Ellen Austin* found a mysterious ship that disappeared twice.

C h a p t e r

5

Music

Unit 17

Louis Armstrong

A Listen to the talk on page 84 again. Then, write the answers to the questions.

1 What was the title of the famous song Louis Armstrong recorded?

____

2 Where was Louis Armstrong born?

____

3 What musical instrument did Louis Armstrong learn to play?

____

4 Why did Louis Armstrong start doing scat singing?

____

5 When did Louis Armstrong die?

____

B Use the words in the box to complete the sentences. You may need to change the forms of the words.

lyric sheet	scat singing	birthplace	drop out of	unfortunate

1 ________________ does not use actual words, but the singer just makes various sounds.

2 Jane's ________________ was in the country, but she lives in a big city today.

3 You should study as hard as you can and not ________________ school.

4 Learn the words to the song by studying the ________________.

5 It is ________________ that it is going to snow all day long today.

C **Listen to the talk on page 86 again. Then, fill in the blanks with the correct words.**

1 Ella Fitzgerald's voice was very ________________ to recognize.

2 People often called Ella Fitzgerald "the ________________ of jazz."

3 Ella Fitzgerald made her singing debut at the ________________ in Harlem.

4 Ella Fitzgerald was an accomplished ________________ musician.

5 Ella Fitzgerald sang ________________ and also sang with other famous musical artists.

D **Listen to the talk. Then, complete the outline by filling in the blanks.**

Notes

Scott Joplin

I. Was a famous ⓐ ______________ musician

II. Learned about music in his youth

  i. Learned to play the ⓑ ______________

  ii. Learned about classical music

III. Became a ⓒ ______________ musician

  i. Was called "the ⓓ ______________ of ragtime"

IV. Wrote more than forty ragtime compositions

  i. Wrote *Maple Leaf Rag* and *The Entertainer*

V. Died in 1917

  i. Ragtime became ⓔ ______________ after he died

Unit 18

George Frideric Handel

A **Listen to the talk on page 88 again. Then, write the answers to the questions.**

1 What did George Handel's father want him to become?

____

2 What type of music did George Handel love the most?

____

3 Who did Prince George of Hanover later become?

____

4 What music did the king request to hear several times?

____

5 What was the greatest oratorio George Handel wrote?

____

B **Use the words in the box to complete the sentences. You may need to change the forms of the words.**

rank as	apparent	compose	oboe	choral work

1 Jennifer plays the ______________ in a small orchestra.

2 The singers are going to perform a ______________ at the concert.

3 Johann Sebastian Bach ______________ one of the greatest classical music composers.

4 Martin is planning to ______________ an opera this summer.

5 It is ______________ that the picnic will be canceled because of the rain.

C Listen to the talk on page 90 again. Then, answer T (true) or F (false).

1 ______ George Handel composed *The Messiah* in 1741.

2 ______ The words from *The Messiah* were written by George Handel himself.

3 ______ George Handel took twenty-four years to compose *The Messiah*.

4 ______ The *Hallelujah* chorus is the most recognizable piece from *The Messiah*.

5 ______ King George II stood during the *Hallelujah* chorus because it impressed him.

D Listen to the talk. Then, complete the outline by filling in the blanks.

Notes

Ludwig van Beethoven

I. Was a great classical music composer
  i. Is compared with Bach and Mozart
  ii. Slowly became ⓐ ______________ over time

II. His ⓑ ______________ was performed in 1824
  i. Could not ⓒ ______________ the orchestra
  ii. Stood onstage by the conductor and kept time for the musicians

III. Audience went ⓓ ______________ at the end of the performance

IV. Wrote more than forty ragtime compositions
  i. Beethoven could not hear them
  ii. Could not ⓔ ______________ them since his back was to the crowd
  iii. Caused many musicians to begin crying
  iv. A singer turned Beethoven around so that he could see
  v. The crowd started cheering even louder

Unit 19

Renaissance Musical Instruments

A **Listen to the talk on page 92 again. Then, write the answers to the questions.**

1 When did the Renaissance take place?

____

2 What were some stringed musical instruments people played in the Renaissance?

____

3 What kind of musical instrument was the transverse flute?

____

4 What Renaissance musical instrument was like the trombone?

____

5 What was the shofar?

____

B **Use the words in the box to complete the sentences. You may need to change the forms of the words.**

focus on	similar	remain	a wide range of	hollowed-out

1 We are going to ________________ at the beach for two weeks this summer.

2 He has a musical instrument made from a ________________ animal horn.

3 Try to ________________ your homework so that you can do it properly.

4 At a buffet, you can eat ________________ of various foods.

5 The two friends are so ________________ that people often think they are brothers.

C Listen to the talk on page 94 again. Then, circle the correct answers.

1 Nowadays, most people play (Renaissance / modern) musical instruments.

2 The bagpipe has a very (unique / common) look.

3 People in (Ireland / Scotland) often play the bagpipe.

4 The hammered dulcimer is a (woodwind / stringed) musical instrument.

5 The musician uses (mallets / bows) to play the hammered dulcimer.

D Listen to the talk. Then, match the sentences to make comparisons or contrasts.

Notes

1 Both the sheng and xiao

2 The ancient Chinese had

3 The erhu had two strings,

ⓐ but the pipa had four strings.

ⓑ were ancient Chinese wind instruments.

ⓒ wind instruments as well as stringed instruments.

Unit 20

Movie Soundtracks

A Listen to the talk on page 96 again. Then, write the answers to the questions.

1 Why do movie directors use music in their films?

____

2 What did theaters often do when they played silent movies?

____

3 What is a talkie?

____

4 How many copies has the soundtrack for *The Sound of Music* sold?

____

5 Who is probably the best-known composer of film scores?

____

B Use the words in the box to complete the sentences. You may need to change the forms of the words.

silent movie	film score	amuse	frighten	integral

1 Tim loved the ______________ of the movie so much that he bought the CD.

2 The boy liked to ______________ his younger sister by suddenly jumping out at her.

3 We are going to the theater to watch a ______________ tonight.

4 Mark always ______________ us with his funny jokes.

5 The computer chip is an ______________ part of the computer.

C Listen to the talk on page 98 again. Then, choose the correct answers.

1 John Williams is going to make an appearance with the Boston ________________.

ⓐ Pops ⓑ Orchestra ⓒ Band

2 John Williams is most famous for his ________________.

ⓐ performing ⓑ composing ⓒ conducting

3 John Williams has written the scores for almost all of ________________ movies.

ⓐ George Lucas's ⓑ Oliver Stone's ⓒ Steven Spielberg's

4 The music from ________________ is among the most recognizable of all film music.

ⓐ *Star Wars* ⓑ *Jaws* ⓒ *Raiders of the Lost Ark*

5 It is likely that tickets for the event will ________________.

ⓐ be available ⓑ be expensive ⓒ sell out soon

D Listen to the talk. Then, circle the correct word in each sentence.

Notes

1 John Williams wrote the film scores for (both / neither) *Star Wars* and *Jaws*.

2 The music in *Jaws* is frightening, (so / but) it is epic in *Star Wars*.

3 The music from *Star Wars* is great, (but / and) so is the music from *Jaws*.

memo

memo

We Bring You the World

Mastering Listening Skills Book 2

Mastering Listening Skills Book 2 has several objectives. First, it will help learners improve their English abilities, particularly their listening skills. Next, it will teach them valuable knowledge about a wide range of academic topics. The talks themselves will also entertain learners as they listen to them. Finally, *Mastering Listening Skills Book 2* will help learners prepare for various standardized tests that they may take in the future. For instance, many questions about the talks are similar to those that appear on the iBT TOEFL® Junior and iBT TOEFL® exams. So, by using this book, learners should be able to get higher scores on the tests they take in the future.

For Basic-Level Listeners

Developing Listening Skills Book 1
Developing Listening Skills Book 2

For Intermediate-Level Listeners

Mastering Listening Skills Book 1
Mastering Listening Skills Book 2

Special Features

- **Academic and Entertaining Listening Talks**
  Contains 20 listening talks on all kinds of academic subjects
- **Listening Comprehension and Vocabulary Review Questions**
  Lets listeners test their comprehension of the talks
- **Useful Listening Skills**
  Teaches listeners important skills to make them better at listening
- **Detailed Word List**
  Provides definitions and sample sentences of difficult vocabulary words
- **Comprehensive Workbook**
  Contains extra questions, vocabulary exercises, and listening skill exercises
- **Recordings of Listening Talks**
  Lets listeners improve their listening and pronunciation skills by listening to native speakers